The Poetics of Reading
Textuality and Subjectivity vol. 2

TEXTUALITY AND SUBJECTIVITY VOL 2:
THE POETICS OF READING
Eitel Timm, Kenneth Mendoza, ed.

This second volume in a series of publications on *Textuality and Subjectivity*, a sub-series in *Studies in German Literature, Linguistics, and Culture*, situates the act of critical reading in the context of poietic aesthetics. Concurrent with post-structuralist theories of recent years, the textuality of literary discourse, of history, of media, of philosophy and religion has emerged as a focal point of debate in the humanities. The essays written for this publication examine how questions of the canon, of genres, of transformation of texts may ultimately result in a rethinking of the present epistemological situation. Embodying interdisciplinary approaches of textual "readings," the studies of this second volume in the series draw on a variety of literary figures and critics with the aid of contemporary methodological innovations: from Lessing to Kafka and Celan, from Walter Benjamin to Paul de Man and Derrida.

This study also speaks centrally to the controversial predicament of subjectivity as one of the key terms in current literary and historical scholarship.

With essays by Gerhard Richter, Brent Gowen, Stanley Corngold, Yuan Yuan, John Rice and Paul Malone, Cezar Ornatowski, Kenneth Mendoza, Louis Helbig, Paulo Medeiros.

Eitel Timm teaches at the Vancouver Waldorf School,
Kenneth Mendoza at California State University, San Marcos.

The Poetics of Reading

Edited by

Eitel Timm
Kenneth Mendoza

C A M D E N   H O U S E

ISBN:1-879751-31-3

Library of Congress Cataloging-in-Publication Data

The Poetics of reading / edited by Eitel Timm, Kenneth Mendoza.
    p.   cm.   -- (Textuality and subjectivity : vol. 2) (Studies in
German literature, linguistics, and culture)
    Includes bibliographical references and index.
    ISBN 1-879751-31-3
    1. Self in literature. 2. Subjectivity in literature.
3. Autopoiesis in literature. 4. Intertextuality. 5. Reader
-response criticism. I. Timm, Eitel Friedrich. II. Mendoza,
    Kenneth. 1953-   . III. Series. IV. Series: Studies in German literature, linguistics, and
culture (Unnumbered)
    PN56.S46P64 1992
    801'/95--dc20   92-29486
                                                CIP

CONTENTS

Foreword

THIS SECOND VOLUME IN A SERIES of publications on *Textuality and Subjectivity* situates the act of critical reading in the context of poetic aesthetics. Concurrent with post-structuralist theories of recent years, the textuality of literary discourse, of history, of media, of philosophy and religion has emerged as a focal point of debate in the humanities. The essays written for this publication examine how questions of the canon, of genres, of transformation of texts may ultimately result in a rethinking of the present epistemological situation. Embodying interdisciplinary approaches of textual "readings," the studies of this second volume in the series draw on a variety of literary figures and critics with the aid of contemporary methodological innovations: from Lessing to Kafka and Celan, from Walter Benjamin to Paul de Man and Derrida.

This study also speaks centrally to the controversial predicament of subjectivity as one of the key terms in current literary and historical scholarship. The intellectual disaffection with representational models privileging unity of discourse has led to the present crisis of thought: it would be ludicrous to assume that a commonly accepted redefinition of the relation between subjectivity and language is at all possible or yet feasible. Rather, as we set out to reevaluate our ranking of subjectivity, text, reading, and representation, a heightened awareness of the historicity of paradigm changes is imperiously called for. Also in this sense are the essays in this study a continuation of the debate begun in the first volume of the present series.

Eitel Timm, Vancouver
Kenneth Mendoza, San Marcos

Gerhard Richter

Difficile Dwellings: Kafka's "The Burrow"

> *Wir graben den Schacht von Babel.*
> — Franz Kafka

> *Tot, Lotte! Eingescharrt der kalten Erde, so eng!*
> — Johann Wolfgang v. Goethe, *Die Leiden des jungen Werther*

> *Es war Erde in ihnen, und sie gruben.*
> — Paul Celan, *Die Niemandsrose*

> Die Schwierigkeiten beim Häuserbauen sind gewaltig.
> — Reinhard Lettau, *Schwierigkeiten beim Häuserbauen*

THE ESSENCE OF THE MODERN and postmodern cultural *Zeitgeist* is exemplified in Kafka's problematization of the self and its relation to the social and conceptual structures in which it is embedded. Although less celebrated than, say, "The Metamorphosis" or *The Trial*, Kafka's late fragment "The Burrow" merits particular critical scrutiny, for in it the problematic of subjectivity is intensified. Written around 1923, "The Burrow" is part of a series of animal parables, including "The Giant Mole" (1914), "Investigations of a Dog" (1922), and "Josephine the Singer or the Mouse People" (1924). The struggles for selfhood enacted by the protagonists in Kafka's earlier texts seem to converge upon the principal figure in this narrative. The first-person narrator, an unspecified animal, whose ceaseless activity revolves around building, guarding and improving his labyrinth-like burrow, meditates on potential threats to the structure in the form of enemies and other disturbances that could "make [their] way in and destroy everything for good" (S 325; B 132).[1] In this essay I shall demonstrate how "The

---

[1] English and German citations for Kafka are provided throughout the text, using the following abbreviations: S (*The Complete Stories*, ed. Nahum Glatzer, New York: Schocken Books, 1978), B (*Beschreibungen eines Kampfes* volume of *Gesammelte Werke. Taschenbuchausgabe in sieben Bänden*, ed. Max Brod, Frankfurt: Fischer, 1983), LF (*Letters to Felice*, trans. James Stern and Elisabeth Duckworth, New York: Schocken Books, 1973), BF (*Briefe an Felice*, eds. Erich Heller and Jürgen Born, Frankfurt: Fischer, 1967), DI (*Diaries 1910 To 1913*, trans. Joseph Kresh, New York: Schocken Books, 1949), DII (*Diaries 1914-1923*, trans. Martin Greenberg, New York:

Burrow" may be profitably read in light of current subjectivity debates.[2] Before embarking on this analysis, however, it behooves us to stake out briefly the appropriate critical territory.

While contemporary critical theories have tended to cluster, in one way or another, around the problematic of subjectivity, the notion of the subject as a coherent individual has come under increasing attack. Indeed, many critics have been inclined to discard the "subject" as an outdated epistemological category. What is meant by "the subject," especially in the area of literary studies, remains veiled behind divergent agendas and presuppositions: "subjectivity" resonates in rather different signifying realms for, say, a feminist psychoanalyst engaged in "cultural studies" and a new historicist. What can be distilled, however, from such heterogeneous discourses is a renouncement of the belief in a traditional, self-identical subject. Critical theorists argue that new approaches are needed to examine the epistemological structures underlying the autonomous, coherent, self-governing individual posited by Western tradition. Although it remains difficult

---

Schocken Books, 1949), T (*Tagebücher* volume of the *Gesammelte Werke,* op. cit.). I have silently modified some of the English translations in order to render the German more precisely and have translated German and French secondary citations into English.

[2] Earlier readings have tended to neglect the specificity of the subjectivity struggle in "The Burrow." In Walter Sokel's paradigmatic symbolic reading, "The Burrow" metamorphoses into "a subterrestial, labyrinth-like fortress of extreme loneliness and high-handedness, of absolute self-indulgence," a hedonistic reading that sees the self as mimetically reflecting an empirical/psychological reality. *Franz Kafka - Tragik und Ironie: Zur Struktur seiner Kunst.* (München, Wien: Langen, Müller, 1964), p. 371. Wilhelm Emrich's reading appears to be somewhat more self-conscious in treating *textual* selfhood in "The Burrow": "Kafka's 'Burrow' reflects [the] delusion of consciousness in the human race, a delusion from which man never escapes." *Franz Kafka: A Critical Study of his Writings,* (New York: Ungar, 1968), p. 224. In a largely biographical approach ("closely interrelated with the rest of Kafka's life"), Heinz Politzer assumes that with the burrow "Kafka was dreaming of his return to the womb." *Franz Kafka: Parable and Paradox,* (Ithaca: Cornell University Press, 1962), p. 332. Biographical approaches also inform the essays by Verne Snyder, "Kafka's 'Burrow': A Speculative Analysis," *Twentieth Century Literature* 27:2 (1981), Britta Maché, "The Noise of the Burrow: Kafka's Final Dilemma," *The German Quaterly* 55:4 (1982), and Andrea Reiter, "Franz Kafkas autobiographische Erzählungen 'Der Bau' und 'Die Forschungen eines Hundes': Selbstanalyse oder Gleichnis?" *Sprachkunst* 18 (1987), who read the "The Burrow" largely as allegorizing the decaying Kafka and the resulting autobiographical strains within the text. Gerhard Kurz's general assessment is that the "story is [...] an allegory of human existence." *Traum-Schrecken: Kafkas literarische Existenzanalyse,* (Stuttgart: Metzler, 1980), p. 193. Bert Nagel's coda is similar: "'The Burrow' deals with consequent isolation, with the loneliness with oneself, finally with confrontation with the absolute." *Kafka und die Weltliteratur,* (München: Winkler, 1983), p. 370. For Gilles Deleuze and Félix Guattari, "The Burrow" assumes the status of one of several metonymic access roads to Kafka: "How to enter Kafka's work? [...] The burrow of the story with the same title seems to have but one entrance; the animal only thinks of the possibilty of a second one for purposes of surveillance." *Pour une Littérature Mineur,* (Paris: Les Editions de Minuit, 1975), p. 7.

to state a precise meaning of the term "subject," useful working definitions given by Paul Smith and Jean-Luc Nancy illustrate contemporary theoretical usage:

> And thence the commonly used term "subject" will be broken down and will be understood as the term inaccurately used to describe what is actually the series or the conglomeration of *positions*, subject-positions, provisional and not necessarily indefeasible, into which a person is called momentarily by the discourses and the world that he/she inhabits ...
> [My sense is] (a) that the term "subject" is best understood as the equivalent of what I call colligated *subject-positions* and (b) that the term "individual" is ideologically designed to give the false impression that human beings are free and self-determining, or that they are constituted by undivided and controlling consciousnesses.[3]

> The dominant definition of the philosophical (or "metaphysical") *subject* is to my way of thinking the one proposed by Hegel: "that which is capable of maintaining within itself its own contradiction."[4]

Theoretical skepticism vis-à-vis the subject and especially the writing subject, the Author, has assumed unprecedented dimensions. Roland Barthes postulates the death of the writing subject in his seminal essay, "The Death of the Author," as follows:

> We can never know, for the good reason that writing is the destruction of every voice, every origin. Writing is that neuter, that composite, that obliquity into which our subject flees, the black-and-white where all identity is lost, beginning with the very identity of the body that writes.[5]

Finally, Barthes advocates the death of the writing subject in favor of the reader:

> Classical criticism has never been concerned with the reader; for that criticism, there is no other man in literature than the one who writes. We are no longer so willing to be the dupes of such antiphrases, by which a society proudly recriminates in favor of precisely what it discards, ignores, muffles, or destroys; we know that in order to restore writing to its future, we must reverse the myth: the birth of the reader must be requited by the death of the Author.[6]

On this view, writing is no longer the privileged site of the coherent, unproblematical individual; the writing subject has been supplanted by the reader, displaced in a *tabula rasa*. This view leads Jacques Derrida to speak of "the absence of

---

[3] Paul Smith, *Discerning the Subject*, (Minneapolis: University of Minnesota Press, 1988), p. xxxv.

[4] Jean-Luc Nancy, "Introduction," *Who Comes after the Subject?*, eds. Eduardo Cadava, Peter Connor, and Jean-Luc Nancy (New York: Routledge, 1991), p. 6.

[5] Roland Barthes, "The Death of the Author," *Contemporary Critical Theory*, ed. Dan Latimer, (San Diego: Hartcourt Brace Jovanovich, 1989), p. 54f.

[6] Ibidem, p. 59.

every empirically determinable 'subject'."[7] Hand in hand with the disappearance of the writing subject goes the problematization of a related notion which has traditionally been regarded as stable: writing as an element of the expressive mode. "First of all we can say that today's writing has freed itself from the dimension of expression. Referring only to itself [...] writing is identified with its own unfolded exteriority," claims Michel Foucault.[8] Writing is thus reinterpreted as self-reflexive, primarily concerned with its own signifying activities at the expense of the signified and the referent. Foucault thus proposes to "re-examine the privileges of the subject," skeptically "call[ing] back into question the absolute character and founding role of the subject."[9] What is needed, then, is an analysis of "the subject as a variable and complex function of discourse."[10]

The critical attack on the subject has not gone without its counter currents. Several tendencies in contemporary theory indicate a renewed interest in salvaging the subject.[11] One of the central issues in Fredric Jameson's latest work, for instance, is the position and condition of the subject, a subject that seeks to cognitively map itself in, and in opposition to, the breakdown of signifying chains. The fragmented subject is seen as reclaiming the organizational structures governing perception. Cognitive mapping is a process constituted by a series of psychological transformations through which the subject acquires, codes, and stores, recalls, and manipulates information about the nature of its environment. Jameson emphasizes the subject's need "to locate itself, to organize its immediate surroundings perceptually, and cognitively to map its position in a mappable external world."[12] He thus proposes the theoretical implementation of an innovative mode of self-representation, an affirmative charting of the subject through a heightened

---

[7] Jacques Derrida, *Margins of Philosophy*, trans. Alan Bass, (Chicago: University of Chicago Press, 1982), p. 315.

[8] Michel Foucault, "What is an Author?," *Textual Strategies*, ed. Josué Harari, (Ithaca: Cornell University Press, 1979), p. 142.

[9] Ibidem, p. 158.

[10] Ibidem.

[11] See for example John Smith's review essay on the books of three critics arguing on behalf of the self (Corngold, Dallmayr, Frank): "Among the literally oxymoronic experiences of the last century that both 'chastened' and 'enriched' our conception of the subject must be counted the German literary and philosophical tradition. Readings of that tradition and its reception have in fact been at the core of both the deconstruction and the reconstruction of the subject. The works under review here can be understood as contributions to such readings. They argue that the German tradition offers us less an ultimate dissolution of the category of subjectivity than a more complex concept of individuality that-in a way yet to be examined-transcends its deconstruction." "The Transcendance of the Individual," *Diacritics* 19:2 (1989), p. 82.

[12] Fredric Jameson, "Postmodernism, or, the Cultural Logic of Late Capitalism," *New Left Review* 146 (1984), p. 83f.

awareness of its cognitive and spatial position in externality. This process enables the subject to organize itself and make sense of the world around it.[13]

Critical theories negating the writing subject are productively set in opposition to approaches affirming the possibility of locating the self with respect to external coordinates. A juxtaposition of these viewpoints produces rifts and fissures, a staked theoretical space in which a new conceptualization of the self begins to unfold. I shall argue that Kafka's narrative "The Burrow" textually reenacts the existential struggle of the writing subject. The animal's ceaseless construction of its burrow in an attempt to defend itself against potential dissolution allegorizes the struggle of the signifying subject to constitute itself through rhetorical maneuvers while confronting the potentially non-referential quality of language. In this way Kafka's text suggests the possibility of mapping the self through writing while at the same time problematizing such an endeavor by alluding to the potential dissolution of the cognitive coordinate system. The oppositions of determinacy and indeterminacy, of presence and deferral of meaning, foreground the vacillation of the subject between affirmation and dislocation.

Eloquent evidence has been marshalled in support of the view that one of the dominant concerns in Kafka is writing itself, rendering his texts largely as self-referential treatments of their own concrete linguisticality and material mode of rhetorical production. In Stanley Corngold's formulation:

> Kafka's most marked contribution to modern art and culture is to the way in which the subject of writing has become Writing, the way in which reflection on the act of writing has become ontological, not psychological, ranging from metaphysical reference to technical aspects of production.[14]

Kafka's writing is a metaphor of itself, an "imaging [of] the scriptive process," an allegory of writing and reading.[15] This self-reflexivity is for Kafka a way to write the self, to become a subject. In a diary entry from Christmas Eve, 1910, he concludes a description of the topography of his desk, writing:

> Wretched, wretched, and yet with good intentions. It is midnight, but since I have slept very well, that is an excuse only to the extent that by day I would have written nothing. The burning electric light, the silent house, the darkness outside, the last waking moments, they give me the right to write even if it be only the most miserable stuff. And this right I use hurriedly. That's the person I am [Das bin ich also] (DI 38f.; T 27).

---

[13] Roger Downs and David Stea, eds., *Image and Environment: Cognitive Mapping and Spatial Behavior*, (Chicago: Aldine, 1973).

[14] Stanley Corngold, *Franz Kafka: The Necessity of Form*, (Ithaca: Cornell University Press, 1988), p. 2, n 5.

[15] Charles Bernheimer, *Flaubert and Kafka: Studies in Psychopoetic Structure*, (New Haven: Yale University Press, 1982), p. 188.

Kafka here identifies his being with writing. Writing is a fleeting right, an opportunity to be seized quickly in order to achieve, at least momentarily, subjective identity. In a 1913 letter to Felice, Kafka agonizes: "If only I could write! I am consumed with the desire to do so [...]. I don't think you have properly taken in that writing is my only possibility for inner existence [innere Daseinsmöglichkeit]" (LF 245; BF 367). Other confidences further bespeak Kafka's conviction that in the absence of writing, existence is called into question: "Tomorrow I shall start to write again, I want to delve into it [hineinreiten] with all my strength; when not writing I feel myself being pushed out of life by unyielding hands" (LF 116; BF 197). Writing becomes for Kafka an existential necessity "if one doesn't want to give oneself over to total despair" (LF 76; F 142), an ontic commitment: "My life consists, and basically always has consisted, of attempts at writing" (LF 20; BF 65); "I can't even cope with myself, except when I am writing" (LF 272; BF 402). The desire to write the self even assumes erotic dimensions: "[T]o have an urge, an urge, a screaming urge to write! [Lust, Lust, Lust, eine schreiende Lust zum Schreiben in sich haben]" (LF 132; BF 218).[16] For Kafka writing is akin to the essence of being: "Dearest, this too, and perhaps this above all, you do not take into account sufficiently in your considerations, though we have written a great deal about it: namely, that writing is actually the good part of my nature [mein eigentliches gutes Wesen]. If there is anything good about me, it is that" (LF 275; BF 404). Scripture is viewed as enabling existence, as the privileged medium of the self-constructing subject, because, as Walter Benjamin writes apropos of Kafka, "writing [...] is not writing but life."[17] Writing becomes the constitutive metaphor of being-in-the-world, the material signification of the self. The narrating subject engages in a process of self-constitution in and through language. As Nicolae Babuts formulates these dynamics, "there is no doubt that speakers have to define themselves through language [...]. [I]n the process, the speaking subject does attain self-realization. [Textual patterns] re-form their original tension and become affirmations or evidence on behalf of the self."[18]

The dominant metaphor of "The Burrow" is writing. The scratching and digging activities of the animal serve as an allegory of the writing process. As Corngold points out, such a paradigmatic reading "is strengthened by the link between the scratching, digging activity (*scharren*) of the burrowing creature and the act of writing (*schreiben*); both verbs derive from the common Indo-European

---

[16] Concerning the eroticism of writing in Kafka, see Detlef Kremer, *Kafka: Die Erotik des Schreibens*, (Frankfurt: Athenäum, 1989).

[17] Walter Benjamin, *Walter Benjamin/Gersholm Scholem: Briefwechsel 1933-1940*, (Frankfurt: Suhrkamp, 1980), p. 166.

[18] Nicolae Babuts, "Text: Origins and Reference," *PMLA* 107 (1992), p. 67.

root *sker*."[19] A further etymological relation between "graben" (digging) and "schreiben" (writing) consists in the the Greek verb "graphein," writing as engraving, a reference that Kafka playfully expands upon.[20] Thus the connection between "bauen" (constructing) and the process of writing the self becomes evident.[21] The preeminent metaphor of the text suggests that what is at stake here is more than the construction of an inhabitable dwelling; it is an attempt at the construction of existence through writing, an allegory of Kafka's *Schriftstellersein* or being-as-a-writer, a kind of meta-metaphor for the struggle of the writing/written subject.

It is the frenzied construction activity of the animal that allegorizes the subject's desire to write the self. Digging serves as a metaphor of writing; the animal states that "my style of digging makes very little noise" (S 359; B 165). In an attempt to write the self, the act of writing becomes the joyous climax of creation: "[M]y first joy in labor found riotous satisfaction there in the labyrinthine burrow which at the time seemed to me the crown of all burrows" (S 331; B 138). Enthusiasm accompanies this process of creation, "for I still have a certain sentiment about this first achievement [Erstlingswerk] of mine" (S 332; B 138). The term "Erstlingswerk," a technical term referring to a writer's first work, conjures up the image of the writer and the written in their concrete materiality. This perpetual self-construction is a struggle of life against death, and threatening disturbances have to be met "by an instantaneous mobilization of all the resources in the burrow and all the forces of my body and soul — that is self-evident" (S 332; B 139). These threats cannot be sublimated into the transitory guest room of the incidental. The animal's "general map of my burrow" (S 330; B 137) evokes the image of cognitive mapping, the defining cartography of the speaking subject. The narrator's elaborate plan for assigning and reassigning the hierarchy of spaces depending on necessity mirrors the intricate manipulability of locations inhabitable by a coherent self: "thereupon I mark off every third room, let us say, as a reserve storeroom, or every fourth room as a main and every second as an auxiliary storeroom, and so forth" (S 329; B 135f.). The web-like structure of special secure places within the burrow enables the momentary self-identity of the subject: "I lie here in a place secured on every side — there are more than fifty such places in my burrow" (S 327; B 134). Floating between these cognitive poles of self-con-

---

[19] Stanley Corngold, *Franz Kafka: The Necessity of Form*, op. cit., p. 282.

[20] See Detlef Kremer, *Kafka: Die Erotik des Schreibens*, op. cit., p. 141.

[21] Further etymological evidence indicates a relationship between "bauen" (and, by extension, "wohnen," (to live)) and existence. According to Grimm's *Deutsches Wörterbuch*, (Leibzig: Hirzel, 1854ff.), vol. 1, the verb "bauen" in Old High German expressed "sein" (to be). "Ich bin" (I am), or its OHG equivalent *pim*, is etymologically related to "wohnen." The abstraction of being derives from the image of "living," a verb that in English still signifies both inhabiting and being (pp. 1170ff.).

tainment, the subject can organize and reorganize itself: "I can always rearrange accordingly [Neuordnungen vornehmen]" (S 328; B 135), a vital skill in the confusing galaxy of signifiers, the "densest traffic" of the subject's externality (S 334; B 141). The animal finds his happiness in reflecting upon "how steadfast a protection my burrow" can be (S 335; B 141). The written coordinate grid thus "fastens" the subject as it moves through the space of signification. On it, the subject attempts to create for itself "the loveliest imaginable place of residence," (S 346; B 152) in which it is possible "to be intimately familiar with all passages and directions" (S 326; B 133).[22]

Yet writing the self is also a risk, a "Risiko" (B 138). The animal realizes that his construct has "so many weaknesses imposed by nature" (S 332; B 139). Struggling ceaselessly with the inadequacies of language, the subject bemoans the incompleteness of its house-of-being (a recurrent image in the text). The burrow is not always safe, it can at any time fall prey to the insufficiency of its construction and design. Theoretical considerations of modes of construction and methodology do not help; they threaten the self and are thus counterproductive: "And with that I lose myself in technical speculations" (S 339; B 145). Yet, digging/writing without any design is equally ineffective in the process of self-construction: "[A]nd though I do some digging I do it at random; naturally that has no effect, and the hard work of digging and the still harder work of refilling and leveling [the earth] is labor lost" (S 344; B 150). The only apparent solution to this predicament is to engage in self-reflexive activity, a writerly *l'art pour l'art*, in which one is led to "start to dig drearily and defiantly, simply for the sake of digging [...] almost like the small fry who burrow either without any sense at all or simply because they eat the soil" (S 349; B 155). Embedded in this realization is the impasse of rewriting, the difficulty of an aesthetically oriented re-vision: "the final improvements, which demand a stricter attention, I can hardly achieve at all" (S 350; B 156). Writing the self is presented as something like the motion of a pendulum vacillating between construction and dispersal, between affirmation and dissolution. The writing process serves as a tool for self-mapping which, because of the equivocalness of linguistic representation, poses a threat of dissolution to the writing subject. A struggle is enacted against the insufficiencies of writing and the instability of an existence constructed in and through text.

---

[22] Cf. Kremer's formulation of such a process in Kafka in general: "In this [...] process of transformation every letter is important, for every letter is a part of the self," *Kafka: Die Erotik des Schreibens*, op. cit., p. 131. Clayton Koelb, "The Lived Rhetoric of Franz Kafka," *Journal of the Kafka Society of America* 10 (1986), writes that Kafka "can only make himself into a text [...], can never [...] experience himself apart from structures of language" (p. 67).

The narrative indicates that the inhabitant of the burrow and the burrow itself are inseparable.[23] The burrow appears as a physical extension of the written self, productively conceptualized as the subject's written body: "At such times I feel as if I were not standing in front of my house but rather in front of myself" (S 334; B 140). Rhetorically addressing the tunnels and chambers of his burrow, the animal advances: "You belong to me, I to You, we are united; what can harm us?" (S 342; B 149). There is "no need for me even to take thought to know what the burrow means to me; I and the burrow belong so indissolubly together [...] for nothing can part us for long" (S 340; B 147). The creature refers to his burrow as "my fortress which can never belong to anyone else in any way, and which is so essentially mine [...] my blood will ebb away here in my own soil and not be lost" (S 340; B 146). Indeed, the "pain" of the burrow is experienced by the narrator as his own, "the vulnerability of the burrow has made me vulnerable, its wounds hurt as if they were mine" (S 355; B 161). Assuming the material perspective of the bodily burrow the narrator reveals, "I am [...] completely grown together with the rest of the forest ground" (S 333; B 139). The passageways of the burrow function as an extension of the narrator's own respiratory system, "provid[ing] me with good fresh air to breathe" and "offer[ing] me the possibility of extensive scenting" (S 326; B 133). Breathing takes place deep inside the burrow/body, where "[I] breathe in deeply the tranquility of my house" (S 329; B 136). The narrator experiences vulnerability in the areas in which his burrow is vulnerable: "at that point in the dark moss I am mortal" (S 325; B 132). The description of the entrance to the burrow as "positively tensed up [förmlich verkrampft]" (S 340; B 146) further evidences the vital connection between animal and burrow.

Kafka's depiction of the self-mapping endeavor is complicated by the creature's identification with the dwelling that he has constructed. In the process of producing an external coordinate system with which to map his position in the outside world, the animal has come to view the burrow as an extension of himself. The struggling subject's inextricable bond with its written body suggests that the process of self-construction is not merely psychological nor simply epistemological but also ontologically material.[24] In this way the subject becomes the very

---

[23] Cf. Stanley Corngold: "Hence, the burrow, while an *œuvre*, also exhibits the qualities of a sensate body," *Franz Kafka: The Necessity of Form*, op. cit., p. 284.

[24] For Kafka, the act of writing and the body itself enter an interdependent relationship. The body, then, is a necessary function of the writing process without which scripture would be impossible. Having just completed *The Judgement*, Kafka enters into his diary on September 23, 1912: "*Only in this way* can writing be done, only with such coherence, with such a complete opening out of the body and the soul" (Kafka's emphasis; DI 276; T 214); on February 11, 1913, he writes: "This is necessary because the story came out of me like a real birth, covered with filth and slime, and only I have the hand that can reach to the body itself and the strength of desire to do so" (DI 178; T 217). Emphasizing the corporeal dimension of writing, Kafka intertwines the axes of

text that it has produced in its efforts to find cognitive bearings through the writing process. The textual burrow thus becomes the material matrix in which the self is read and defined. This image thematizes a basic assumption of ontological hermeneutics, namely that in phenomenological perception a critical sensibility to contextual structures surrounding the phenomenon to be interpreted must be taken into account (indeed, Martin Heidegger would argue that the nature of all inquiry is inexorably intertwined with an understanding of the interpretative act). As Heidegger casts it:

> That wherein *Dasein* already understands itself in this way is always something with which it is primordially familiar. This familiarity with the world does not necessarily require that the relations which are constituitive for the world should be theoretically transparent. However, the possibility of giving these relations an explicit ontologico-existential Interpretation, is grounded in this familiarity with the world; and this familiarity, in turn, is constitutive for *Dasein*, and goes to make up *Dasein*'s understanding of Being. This possibility is one which can be seized upon explicitly in so far as *Dasein* has set itself the task of giving a

---

semantic unfolding and external materiality to evoke something like a materially construed signifying activity. It is this bodily materiality that serves Kafka as a matrix for his reflections on writing and meaning.

Lehmann states apropos of the problem of writing and the body in Kafka: "Reading Kafka's entire œuvre before this background would probably reveal the author's singular insistence on the bodily and mental reality of the act of writing." "Der buchstäbliche Körper: Zur Selbstinszenierung der Literatur bei Franz Kafka," *Der junge Kafka*, ed. Gerhard Kurz, (Frankfurt: Suhrkamp, 1984), p. 240.

Taking his point of departure from the assumption that in Kafka in general one finds "the transformation of the body into a piece of writing," Gerhard Neumann proceeds to do pioneering work on the issue of body and writing in Kafka. "Schreibschrein und Strafapparat: Erwägungen zur Topographie des Schreibens," *Bild und Gedanke: Festschrift für Gerhart Baumann zum 60. Geburtstag*, ed. Günter Schnitzler, (München, Fink, 1980), p. 398.

On the problematic of a writerly being as it relates to Kafka's rhetorical models, see Reinhard Lettau's discussion of Kafka's narrative models in *Zerstreutes Hinausschaun: Vom Schreiben in direkter Nähe oder in der Entfernung von Schreibtischen*, (Frankfurt: Fischer, 1982): "Kafka's writing literally ends with the attempt at not contradicting hopelessness by the fact that one has had the energy to identify it" (p. 190). On Kafka's writerly modes of being, see further Stanley Corngold, *The Fate of the Self: German Writers and French Theory*, (New York: Columbia University Press, 1986).

The process of constructing the self materially (and its challenges) are in turn subjected to the demands of one of the leitmotifs in Kafka, that of legitimizing existence. Hence the subject takes great pains to bring forth writing and its rhetoricity as an affirmation of its concrete existence. By the same token, scripture must justify its existence by invoking its relation to the subject: "[A]nd I am both angered and touched when, as sometimes happens, I lose myself for a moment in my own maze, and the work seems to be still doing its best to justify its existence to me after all" (S 333; B 139).

primordial Interpretation for its own Being and for the possibilities of that Being, or indeed for the meaning of Being in general.[25]

What is at stake here is the difference between conceptualizing local or specific understandings of existence and the disclosures of context, two interdependent aspects in Heidegger's investigation of *Dasein*. The animal depends on the burrow to provide the context enabling him to perform an interpretative act concerning the self; he is capable of mapping himself only within the contextual structure of his burrow. However, the phenomenological difference between self and non-self here becomes blurred in so far as both are interrelated. Through the absence of a concrete difference between the animal and his burrow, the narrator's ability to become a self-interpreting being is problematized, for, according to Heidegger, the hermeneutical understanding of a phenomenon depends on the productive reading of its context. The burrowing creature faces the aporia of "reading" himself without access to a context qualitatively different from himself. In this way the bodily burrow exhibits the face of Janus, on the one hand providing a space in which the self may unfold, on the other hand rendering hermeneutical insights into the essence of that self impossible.

The ever present threat of the dreaded "Other" poses yet another significant challenge to the burrowing creature in his endeavor to establish selfhood. The animal lives in constant fear of possible attacks by the Other: "I am living in peace in the inmost chamber of my house, and meanwhile the enemy is digging his way slowly and steadily straight toward me" (S 326; B 133). The general struggle of affirmation and dispersal in this text is thus underscored and intensified in the discourse of the battle with the Other. Anticipating a "serious attack" (S 332; B 138), even a "destructive battle [Vernichtungskampf]" (S 335; B 141), the animal engages in frequent "reflections on defensive measures" (S 328; B 135). The animal lives in horror of the gaze of the Other, anxiously inquiring: "[W]ould he not at least want to see the burrow?" (S 338; B 144). Thus, the gaze of the Other is constructed as a feared medium of hostile power. In the animal's mind, the destabilizing Other is endowed with unusual "strength," "haste," and a "furious lust for work" (S 354; B 160), a kind of idealization reflecting the desired self-image of the narrating animal.[26] The only recourse the animal sees, then, is

---

[25] Martin Heidegger, *Being and Time*, trans. John Macquarrie and Edward Robinson, (New York: Harper and Row, 1962), p. 119.

[26] As Lorna Martens suggests: "In Kafka's fiction generally, the 'other,' inasmuch as it is imagined at all, becomes a purely self-reflexive category." "Mirrors and Mirroring: 'Fort/Da' Devices in Texts by Rilke, Hofmannsthal and Kafka," *Deutsche Vierteljahresschrift für Literaturwissenschaft und Geistesgeschichte* 58 (1984), p. 154. This Other, proposes Henrich Henel, is "the animal's [...] repressed sense of futility." "The Burrow, or How to Escape from a Maze," *Franz Kafka*, ed. Harold Bloom, (New York: Chelsea, 1986), p. 132. Winfried Kudszus too agrees that this Other is not an actual presence but rather a psychological mechanism of the narrator. "Verschüttungen in Kafkas 'Der Bau'," *Probleme der Moderne: Studien zur deutschen Literatur*

a fantasy of devouring, of erasing the feared Other: "[C]asting all prudence to the winds, I might in my blind rage leap on him, maul him, tear the flesh from his bones, destroy him, drink his blood, and fling his corpse among the rest of my spoil" (S 337; B 143). Dominance over the Other is here depicted as a complete swallowing, an existential eradication of the difference between self and Other.

And yet the only material evidence for the intersubjective existence of the Other is the humming and "hissing noise," an "almost inaudible hissing" (S 343; B 149). Localization of the fear of the Other "in the inmost" suggests the psycho-pathological construction of an *imaginary* Other. Despite the initially assumed auditory recognition of the self by the Other, the narrator later concludes that the relationship with the Other is merely imaginary: "The more I reflect upon it the more improbable does it seem to me that the animal has even heard me" (S 359; B 164). The animal destabilizes the difference between himself and the imaginary Other, thereby raising the possibility that the feared Other represents the momentary end-result of a shift in subject-positions and not a verifiable entity in intersubjective space: "[I]t may be somebody of my own kind" (S 337; B 143). From a psychoanalytical perspective, it could be argued that the noise signifies something like the return of the repressed (we learn that during the animal's youth, he had already encountered but chosen to ignore the Other), in any case something that happens within the subjective psyche of the narrator. The battle of different subject-positions manifest here in the ever present fear of an imaginary Other further illustrates the struggle between the desired presence of a self-identical, coherent subject mappable in the external world and a destabilized, fragmented, pathologically disturbed self.[27]

von Nietzsche bis Brecht. Festschrift für Walter Sokel, eds. Benjamin Bennett, Anton Kaes, and William Lillyman, (Tübingen: Niemeyer, 1983). Concerning Brod's unhelpful claim that Kafka wanted to finish the fragment by having the animal fight with the intruder, Kudszus writes: "Would such an ending not remain on the surface of the textual structure? For a final decisive battle between the animal and the enemy would presuppose boundaries of identity that are deconstructed [abgebaut] in the text" (p. 314). Clayton Koelb points in a similar direction: "The world leaves open the possibility of a rhetorical slide by which the narrator's concern with his burrow merges with an anxiety regarding the constructed enemy [...]. Both these constructions are arguably aspects of the narrator's self." *Kafka's Rhetoric: The Passion of Reading*, (Ithaca: Cornell University Press, 1989), p. 245.

[27] Beatrice Wehrli views the hissing noise and the problem of the Other as follows: "Time and again circular reflections prevent the animal from being released from its anxiety and finding its peace." "Monologische Kunst als Ausdruck moderner Welterfahrung: zu Kafkas Erzählung 'Der Bau'," *Jahrbuch der Deutschen Schiller-Gesellschaft* 25 (1981), p. 440. Henrich Henel, op. cit., and Hermann Weigand, "Franz Kafka's 'The Burrow' ('Der Bau'): An Analytical Essay," *PMLA* 87 (1972), see the hissing noise as either imaginary or the animal's own breathing. Politzer too locates the noise "in the animal's imagination" (p. 330). Among those who read the hissing as evidence of an actual Other, Gerhard Kurz suggests that the "hissing is the noise of the snake, for Kafka simultaneously a symbol of sexuality and of death." *Traum-Schrecken: Kafkas literarische Existenzanalyse*, op. cit., p. 193. Marjorie Gelus, "Notes on Kafka's 'Der Bau': Problems with

It is not the "pure" Other as an object that seems to account for the narrator's fantasies. Rather, the narrating subject creates the Other as a function of its own desire. The Other momentarily occupies the space of the excess of desire, the X, that can take any shape, assume any form. The Other is the recipient of the subject's projections, a temporary screen imaging the reality of what is finally *someone else's* focused desire. According to René Girard, such a desire "can always be portrayed by a simple straight line which joins subject and object."[28] In this way the feared animal becomes the locus of the narrating subject's desire.

Referring to Lacan, Julia Kristeva suggests that a subject's existence is dependent upon its identification with an ideal Other. This process of identification aids the subject in constructing its preferred self-image. Through this idealized relationship it becomes part of the Other; it is woven into a symbolic interdependence. It is this relationship that empowers the subject to establish imaginary objects of desire:

> Transferred to the Other [...] as to the very place from which he is seen and heard, the [...] subject does not have access to that Other as an object, but as to the very possibility of the perception, distinction and differentiation that allows one to see. That ideal is nevertheless a blinding, non-representational power - sun or ghost.[29]

According to Kristeva, the Other is a (potentially hostile) means to construct the ideal self. Viewed from this perspective, the subject in Kafka's text appears to depend on the Other in its attempt to construct the ideal self. The ideal Other is both needed and feared. Although denied access to the Other, the animal is empowered by its imaginary existence, enabled to conceive of the self, at least momentarily, as a self-identical consciousness. The Other, then, is understood "not

---

Reality," *Colloquia Germanica* 15 (1982), sees in the hissing noise an "objective existence" (p. 107); overall, she desires to objectify the world of the burrow and ascribe to it a psycho-social truth-functional value: "We have seen that there is, indeed, an objective world" (ibid.). Allen Thiher, *Franz Kafka: A study of the Short Fiction*, (Boston: Twayne, 1990), reads the noise as a stimulus for scientific investigation (p. 14). For earlier interpretations of the noise, mainly denying its independent existence, see Schillemeit's discussion, "Der einzelne und sein Werk ('Der Bau')," *Kafka-Handbuch in zwei Bänden*, ed. Hartmut Binder, (Stuttgart: Kroner, 1979),vol. 2, p. 394f. One is inclined to differ with Dorrit Cohn's statement that the noise "will destroy this idyllic state," considering the existential torment the animal experiences from the very beginning of the text. *Transparent Minds*, (Princeton: Princeton University Press, 1978), p. 196. Stanley Corngold proposes: "The sound has a clear-cut functional identity. It provokes in the narrator a sense of the futility of all his attempts to shore against ruin by continuing to dig, to write." *Franz Kafka: The Necessity of Form*, op. cit., p. 285.

[28] René Girard, *Deceit, Desire, and the Novel: Self and Other in Literary Structure*, trans. Yvonne Freccero, (Baltimore: Johns Hopkins University Press, 1965), p. 2.

[29] Julia Kristeva, *The Kristeva Reader*, ed. Toril Moi, (New York: Columbia University Press, 1986), p. 253.

as a 'pure signifier' but as the very space of metaphorical shifting."[30] For the animal, the Other becomes the double-edged metaphor of his mirrored self. He depends on the Other as a reflective trajectory of his subject-positions but ultimately is denied the full identification with the Other necessary for the establishment of a coherent and coordinated self-image. This predicament reflects precisely what is at stake for the subject throughout Kafka's text, namely the ontological tension between self-construction and self-loss.

The burrowing animal's troubled imaginary relation to the intruder foregrounds his predicament: the conflict-producing impulse to fulfill desire in and through the Other whom he fears and hates. According to Girard, "[o]nly someone who prevents us from satisfying a desire which he himself has inspired in us is truly an object of hatred. The person who hates first hates himself for the secret admiration concealed by his hatred."[31] Although the idealized Other is still secretly desired, it is transformed into "a shrewd and diabolical enemy; he tries to rob the subject of his most prized possessions; he obstinately thwarts his most legitimate ambitions."[32] The reaffirmation of the self is attempted through the condemnation of the Other as the emblem of all that is hostile to the maintenance of a satisfied, intelligible, and non-threatened self.[33]

---

[30] Ibidem, p. 254.

[31] René Girard, op. cit., p. 10f.

[32] Ibidem, p. 11.

[33] This thematic of the Other may also be productively cast in Lacanian language. According to Slavoj Zizek's analysis of Lacanian theory, *Looking Awry: An Introduction to Jacques Lacan through Popular Culture*, (Cambridge, MA: MIT Press, 1991), it is imperative that the object occupy the empty place of the Thing. On this view, the temporary screen of projected desire must appear to have always already been there, "not placed there by us but *found there as an 'answer of the real'*"(p. 33). Although any object can serve as the screen of desire, it is critical that the subject be under the illusion that the source of the fascination lies in the object itself (ibid.): "But why, we may ask, can the performative effect take place only on condition that it is overlooked? Why does the disclosure of the performative mechanism necessarily ruin its effect? Why, to paraphrase *Hamlet*, is the king (also) a thing? Why must the symbolic mechanism be hooked onto a 'thing,' some piece of the real? The Lacanian answers is, of course: because the symbolic field is in itself always already barred, crippled, porous, structured around some extimate kernel, some impossibility. The function of the 'little piece of the real' is precisely to fill out the place of this void that gapes in the very heart of the symbolic" (p. 33). That little piece of the real is precisely the hissing noise necessary for the perpetuation of the narrating subject's projection of the Other. The hissing noise becomes the answer of the real. Whether or not it really exists becomes secondary; what is important is that the subject takes that sound as the fragment of an affirmation of the Other's realness. Such a "paranoid construction enables us to escape the fact that 'the Other does not exist' (Lacan) — that it does not exist as a consistent, closed order — to escape the blind, contingent automatism, the constituitive stupidity of the symbolic order" (p. 18). Yet it cannot be concluded from this that a mere dismantling of the illusion of the Other's existence would allow the subject to see things as they actually are (cf. p. 71). For it is this very illusion that gives form to experiential reality, it is a necessary ingredient in the make-up of our structural existence. The

Viewed from another perspective the struggle of the writing subject to map the self takes the form of a struggle between determinacy and indeterminacy, between the presence and absence of meaning.[34] Since the presence of meaning is critical to the project of establishing selfhood, an examination of the discourse on meaning embedded in the text is in order. Paul de Man's definition of literary language sheds light on the thematic of meaning within the framework of larger hermeneutical strategies:

> For the statement about language, that sign and meaning can never coincide, is what is precisely taken for granted in the kind of language we call literary. Literature, unlike everyday language, begins on the far side of this knowledge; it is the only form of language free from the fallacy of unmediated expression.[35]

It can be argued here that Kafka's language is very much aware of this condition. "The Burrow" is riddled with frequent moments of indeterminacy in which the possibility of meaning is at stake. One of the central strategies of the text, then, is that of foregrounding contradictions serving to frustrate the attempt at achieving hermeneutical closure, at spawning the nexus, in de Man's Language, of meaning and sign. Reflection upon the very title of the text, "The Burrow" ("Der Bau"), which can also be read as "The Construct" ("Das Konstrukt"), suggests a certain irony.[36] As Henry Sussman points out, the construction of a burrow bespeaks a hollowing, not a protrusion.[37] A presence is produced by creating an absence; an earthen dwelling is constructed by the removal of its essence. In this way the

---

absence of the Other thus constitutes the *presence* of an unconscious structuring principle; the non-existence of the other animal is actually inexorably intertwined with the conceptualizing existence of the narrating animal.

[34] Pamela Caughie's statement that the text has no subject seems fascinating, though not entirely warranted: "'The Burrow' is writing without a subject, for the subject is empty outside of the discourse that defines it." "The Death of Kafka: The Birth of Writing," *Newsletter of the Kafka Society of America* 5 (1981), p.14. The confusion here results from the assumption that since no truth-functional Other is foregrounded, the self does not exist either. From that perspective the text would have to write itself without any agency. How can meaning, if we agree that this text generates a meaning process, signify itself outside of an agency through which it travels to become perceptible? It is precisely the problematic of meaning construction of, through, and for the subject that is thematized in this text. Denying a subject its coherence and viewing it as a struggling, fragmented consciouness is not identical with assuming that it does not exist at all. In as far as a text can be said to be, on a certain level, "about" meaning and its deferral, it is implicitly "about" the subjective agent's challenge to cope with that process.

[35] Paul de Man, *Blindness and Insight: Essays in the Rhetoric of Contemporary Criticism*, (Minneapolis: University of Minnesota, 1983), p. 17.

[36] Kafka's preoccupation with the notion of construction becomes apparent in his diary entry of November 21, 1913: "I am on the hunt for constructions" (DI 311; T 242).

[37] Henry Sussman, "The All-Embracing Metaphor: Reflections on Kafka's 'The Burrow'," *Glyph: Johns Hopkins Textual Studies* 1 (1977), p. 101.

fashioning of the burrow brings forth both a production of meaning, of temporary clarity, and at the same time its own complication.[38] The title can thus be said to metonymically anticipate and encapsulate the struggle between construction and dispersal, the subject's temporary attainment of fastenings on a stable coordinate grid and the bottomless fall resulting from a continuous and erratic widening of the meshes of this grid.

From the onset Kafka's writing strategies constitute a discourse on meaning, reenacting its non-unified nature and presenting unresolved contradictions. The narrator speaks, for example, of the existence of the burrow where only a giant hole is visible. The intimation of the burrow's existence is thus destabilized for lack of "objective" perceptual verification. Similarly, the "creatures [Wesen]" of the *innermost* part of the earth are described as *external* enemies and are said to be essentially unrepresentable, although old cultural narratives reportedly describe them: "I have never seen them, but legend tells of them" (S 326; B 133). The exit or existential "Ausweg" from the burrow is actually useless, perhaps even dangerous: "Not even my exit could save me [...] indeed in all probability it would not save me in any case, but rather betray me" (ibid). The climate of the burrow is at once warm and cool (S 327; B 134). The burrow is said to be still, yet the contradiction of this statement follows it immediately: "But the most beautiful thing about my burrow is its stillness. Of course, that is deceptive" (S 327; B 134). The narrator tells us that he has left the burrow, but then concedes that "yet I am not really outdoors" (S 333; B 140). We are told of the animal's desire for specialized technical equipment, yet in the next sentence this statement is negated: "But perhaps not so very desirable after all" (S 339; B 145). The animal insinuates the possession of a tremendous amount of security — "but by no means enough" (S 339; B 146). Indeterminacy of hermeneutics itself is at stake when the reader learns: "But whether unimportant or important, no matter how hard I search, I find nothing, or rather, I find too much" (S 344; B 151). Having devised a new plan of operation, the narrator discloses his emotional reaction equivocally: "The new reasonable plan tempts me and doesn't tempt me" (S 349; B 155). All of a sudden, the animal cannot find the slightest meaning in the plan he has just created (S 352; B 158). The equipment of defense is "remote — or rather not remote (how could that be possible?)" (S 351; B 157). The narrator constantly reinterprets the conditions of his habitat, finding a "complete reversal of things in the burrow," yet "nothing has changed" (S 352; B 158). When finally the intruding Other is putatively identified as one large animal (rather than the previously assumed fleet of "small fry" [Kleinzeug]), the narrator immediately disaffirms himself, intimating that "[m]any signs contradict this" (S 353; B 159). Loud noise is perceived as a quiet hissing (S 354; B 160). Accurate perception

---

[38] Ibidem.

itself is finally problematized: "Had the hissing grown fainter? No, it had grown louder" (S 357; B 163). Temporality is turned on its head: "Between that day and this lie my years of maturity [Mannesalter], but is it not as if there were nothing at all between them?" (S 357; B 162). Finally, indeterminacy culminates in the realization that all that is left is the mere dream of intelligibility, of hermeneutical insight. As in so many of Kafka's texts,[39] the protagonist is made to suffer from the consequences of hermeneutical failure, and this narrator is fully aware of the burden: "and what incalculable consequences might not the smallest accident of that kind [Verhinderung] have for me?" (S 338; B 145). Thus even the grave consequences of a hermeneutical mistake, a slight misreading perhaps, in turn triggers yet another "incalculable," indeterminate complication; the way to meaning seems endlessly deferred. Cause and effect, beginning and end, up and down, are hopelessly entangled in the spiderweb of textuality. Ultimately, the narrator arrives at the cynical conclusion that unmediated expression, straight-forward communicability of and through language is but a hopeless dream: "In my heap of earth I can naturally dream of all sorts of things, even communication [Verständigung], though I know well enough that no such thing exists" (S 358; B164). Incommunicability may be responsible for the potential impossibility of telling this very story, that is to say, the speech act, if it happened, perhaps effected nothing; thus, the last sentence of the text — set off in hyphens — seeks to undermine the previous manipulation of signifiers making up the narrative: "But all remained unchanged" (S 359; B 165). On a certain level, then, "The Burrow" can be read not only as largely indeterminate, but as a commentary on its own indeterminacy.

In foregrounding the struggle between the absence and presence of decidability, Kafka's text mirrors the overarching thematic of the struggling subject. While meaning cannot be said to depend solely on the existence of human agency, the subject is surely a significant vehicle for its disclosure, a site of enunciation through which to travel. The subjective agency, in turn, is not free, but bound and

---

[39] It could be argued, for instance, that the protagonists's suicide in "The Judgment" is a consequence of misreading his father's statement about the "sentence." Similarily, in *The Trial*, Josef K. is entangled in misreadings of his situation (being arrested, his options, guilt, etc.) and suffers the consequences. Embedded in this problematic is the theme of taking metaphors literally. In "The Burrow," too, we have such instances, e.g., the metaphor "etwas unter Dach und Fach bringen" (to successfully complete something, to wrap something up) is literalized for the shelter-seeking subject as "sich unter Dach gebracht zu haben," having a roof over one's head (S 327; B 134). This procedure re-emphasizes the proximity of "wohnen" and "sein."

An actual instance of the vital necessity of close reading is located in the sentence: "And I leave my post of observation and find I have had enough of this outside life [Und ich verlasse meinen Beobachtungsplatz und bin satt des Lebens im Freien]" (S 335; B 142). The absence of one letter, "t," ("satt des Lebens" instead of "statt") bespeaks the crucial operation of meaning, the difference upon which meaning is based. The difference lies between "full of life" [satt des Lebens] and its total opposite, "instead of life" [statt des Lebens]. Thus the reader, like the characters, must perform as thorough and vital a reading of each letter of the text as possible.

situated by its desires, apparati, linguistic representations, and historical contexts. Meaning, then, in a broad sense, is thematized here as a correlative of the subjectivity struggle.

This struggle to establish meaning highlights the binarism of affirmation and negation, of coherence and dispersal, of Work and écriture.[40] How then are we to read Kafka's writing? As the Work of a self-identical, authorial subject possessing a more or less stable meaning, or as textuality endlessly interwoven with other signifying activities and therefore lacking a stable Meaning? The very formulation of this question represents an attempt to locate oneself outside the linguistic imperatives that contain and restrain the space of possible knowledge. Such an endeavor is epistemologically problematic; to speak with Kafka, any question that does not already answer itself in the moment of being posed is unanswerable. What survives, nonetheless, in the margins of such tensions (construction/loss of subject, self/Other, presence/deferral of meaning, Work/écriture) is a wrestling with the process of meaning production, a recurrent preoccupation with the signification of discursive acts. Here the meaning or intelligibility of a sign does not translate unequivocally into a meta-statement of ontological essence, be it subjective, readerly, writerly, cultural, or political. The speaking subject is caught in the sign webs of this constellation, but it is neither dead nor are its activities inconsequential. Rather, as the primary agent through which cognition is facilitated, the subject is critically engaged in the process of meaning construction as well as material and cognitive self-constitution. The poetic subject's complex signifying activities in Kafka's burrow evoke such a process. In this way Kafka's text neither polemically denounces nor blindly affirms the self; it points in the direction of a tendentious reaffirmation of the subject "in a way that avoids the nostalgia for an undeconstructed self."[41]

---

[40] From an editorial perspective, Gerhard Neumann thematizes this irreducible problem in his essay, "Werk oder Schrift? Vorüberlegungen zur Edition von Kafkas Bericht für eine Akademie," *Acta Germanica* 14 (1981): "The ensuing difficulty here is only seemingly an editorial one. Behind the question of the proper classification of the variants hides the question of defining Kafka's texts as either 'scripture' or 'Work,' as 'écriture' which realizes itself in infinite interweavings of written self-affirmation and in which everything is related to everything else; or as 'Work' which in print, cleansed of all its dirt, unfolds itself in perfect form" (p. 5).

[41] John Smith, op. cit., p. 82.

Brent Gowen

The Burden of Our Names

> The paradisiac language of man must have been one of perfect knowledge; whereas later all knowledge is again infinitely differentiated in the multiplicity of language, was indeed forced to differentiate itself on a lower level as creation in name.
>
> Walter Benjamin

> O diese Wege, galaktisch,
> o diese Stunde, die uns
> die Nächte herüberwog in
> die Last unsrer Namen.[1]
>
> Paul Celan

THIS PAPER WILL PARALLEL preoccupations with the naming act of two twentieth-century writers who worked primarily in the German language: the essayist Walter Benjamin and the poet Paul Celan. Given each writer's imprint on modern literature, neither needs much introduction, although baggily one fits both: Born into an assimilated Jewish family (Benjamin in Berlin, 1892; Celan in Romania, 1920), well-educated, a life inured by anti-Semitism and infused by Jewish mysticism, committed suicide (Benjamin 1940; Celan 1970). Celan found more fame in his time, winning several prestigious literary awards (including the Georg Büchner Preis and the Preis der Stadt Bremen) and meeting some public notoriety. But Benjamin, until fifteen years after his death and the first publishing of the posthumous edition of his works and letters, remained little known outside of a small, but brilliant and eclectic circle of colleagues. This circle included Theodor Adorno, Max Horkheimer, Bertolt Brecht, and Stefan George — peers

---

[1] O these ways, galactic.
O this hour, that weighed
nights over for us into
the burden of our names.

(translation by Michael Hamburger)

none of whose strong influences and party lines would Benjamin let direct his versatile intellect.

The extent to which Benjamin's incisive critiques of language and culture influenced the younger Celan is unclear. No evident ties bind, such as those which cord (for example) Benjamin to Gershom Scholem or Celan to Nelly Sachs. Still in his much-discussed "Meridian" speech — a manifesto, of sorts, of his aims as a poet — Celan gestures an affinity for the older writer by quoting a maxim of Malebranche which comes to the surface in Benjamin's essay on Kafka: "Attentiveness is the natural prayer of the soul."[2] Attentiveness to that or to whom appears before one. The attention accorded that or whom one addresses.

In this "Meridian," Celan's evocation of Benjamin immediately precedes a passage in which he sketches a poetics pivoting on attention and address, the two requisites to the naming act:

> The poem becomes — and under what conditions! — a poem of one who [...] perceives, who faces that which appears. Who questions this appearing and addresses it. It becomes dialogue — it is often despairing dialogue.
>
>   Only in the realm of this dialogue does that which is addressed take form and gather around the I who is addressing and naming it. But [that which] has been addressed and [which], by virtue of having been named, has, as it were, become a thou, also brings its otherness along into the present, into this present.[3]

In this passage Celan hails the creative and the *recreative* potential of the naming act: Poetry bids to join in dialogue the namer and the named.

James Lyon particularizes the nature of this bidding by drawing into relationship Celan's dialogic poetics and Martin Buber's I/Thou ontology. Celan's naming-I, explains Lyon, first conjures then connects to the named-Other, who/which in terms of this process (literally) comes into *its* own:

> Every word, every human being, every designation of any kind is potentially a form of this "Other" which the poetic I seeks to engage in dialogue. By articulating phenomena in words, that which is addressed assumes a reality of its own as it begins to constitute the Thou the poem seeks.[4]

---

[2] Paul Celan, "The Meridian," translated by Jerry Glenn, *Chicago Review* (Winter 1978), V. 29, n. 3, p. 37.

[3] Ibidem.

[4] James Lyon, "Paul Celan and Martin Buber: Poetry as Dialogue," *PMLA* (1971), V. 86, n.1, p. 116.

But Celan leaves open and ambiguous the *specific* designation and constitution of this Thou. Who/what is this sought-after Thou, the thus reality-assuming Thou? Is It God? Man? Nature? Self? Only One? Always All?

Another candidate for this Thou remains: language itself. The dialogic drive in Celan's poetry does *not* necessarily confer the namer with God, Man, Nature, or Self. (Celan himself said poems are but and at best messages in a bottle.)[5] But the poetry *does* unavoidably open exchange between those words which the namer has involved in creative dialogue — words thus allowed (even encouraged!) to assume agencies of their own. Exchange, that is, between the words of the namer's own language itself and those of other existing languages which the act of naming has intentionally and accidentally tripped.

Exchange too perhaps between the words of the namer's own language itself and those of a language which the namer can only imagine, a language which the namer imagines has faded from existence, lost but not forgotten. From this remnant perspective, the task of the namer — the poet — would be to recall a special language, and the Thou the namer seeks then would be a memory no longer speakable, a memory perhaps of a more pristine, even paradisiac form of existence.

In naming, we classify that which has taken our attention. We also necessarily direct this attention into some directions and intentions *rather* than into others. Every act of naming must be viewed as exclusionary as well as creative and consequently presents potentials monologic as well as dialogic. And monologic potentials are especially conducive in helping those-who-name appropriate power over those-thus-named. In Celan's and Benjamin's experiences to be named "Jew" rendered one victim; to be named "Jew" was to be monologically abstracted as a "Problem," the monolithic "Solution" to which required the named's restriction or elimination. After 1933, with Hitler in power and brown shirts policing the streets of Berlin, Benjamin was an exile. During the Nazi occupation of Czernowitz, Celan labored in a workcamp; his parents, deported, executed.

Naming inscribes the world, but with *differences* — with classifications of difference which we come to believe are elemental and essential. "You have animals and then you have pets. You have Jews and then you have Gentiles." At once, naming will elbow space for the named to occupy and will culture (often violent) differences in terms of the space named.

In Celanian terms, the naming act is a "Sprachgitter," that grated image central to his work. Within and without Celan's poetry, the "Sprachgitter" is a language

---

[5] In a speech given on the occasion of accepting the literary prize of Bremen in 1958, Celan said: "Since poetry is a form of language and since, therefore, it is essentially a dialogue, it can serve as a message in a bottle, cast on the waters in the belief (not always very hopeful) that it might somewhere, at some time, be washed on land, on a land of the heart perhaps." (translation by Siegbert Prawer).

lattice both enhancing and restricting one's communication with the world, one's placing oneself or being placed in the world. The "Sprachgitter" is a conundrum indicative of all the contradictions found in the realm of language, all the contradictions inherent in the act of naming and that which follows therefrom.

The exposition which follows turns first to several poems of *Die Niemandsrose*, that collection of Celan's poems most overtly concerned with the naming act and with the implications of Jewishness in name and deed, before considering Benjamin's most concentrated discussion of naming, "On Language as Such and on the Language of Man."

Much has been written compellingly on *Die Niemandsrose*. All Celan critics, no matter their personal agendas, must recollect — in brief or at some length — their encounters with that beckoning collection. The characterizations most often forwarded include (in paraphrase) "most accessible of Celan's works," "most Jewish of his works," "most God saken and forsaken." But it is John Felstiner's fecund description of *Die Niemandsrose* in "The Strain of Jewishness" which appears most pertinent: "In *Die Niemandsrose*, Celan sows his verse with more names of people and places, more Jewish terms and quotes, than in any other collection, as if trying to specify a tradition around his individual talent."[6] Celan critics often laud his individual talent for naming, for creating in name a language world according to his own hopes, wishes, lies, dreams, and fears — a world in which what one names is what one gets. But the chief concern here is to examine moments in which Celan indicts rather than invites the naming act.

Felstiner's essays on Celan, particularly those on the matter of translating Celan's poems, implicitly argue the importance (actually the necessity) of lingering mindfully, lovingly over each line of each poem rather than pulling in pieces out of context in an attempt to satisfy one's — the critic's or the translator's — own agenda. So instead of attempting here a synopsis of the pertinence of *Die Niemandsrose* to a discussion of the language act of naming, the following will address primarily one poem, "Soviel Gestirne," before drawing in briefer looks at other poems. Not to claim that "Soviel Gestirne" is "representative" of the collection or even the best "evidence" of this naming notion being advanced, but it does help this commentator to find words to continue writing — a reason for selection which Celan would have approved.

> SOVIEL GESTIRNE, die
> man uns hinhält. Ich war,
> als ich dich ansah — wann? — ,

---

[6] John Felstiner, "Paul Celan: The Strain of Jewishness," *Commentary*, (April, 1985) V.79, n.4, p. 52.

draußen bei
den andern Welten.

O diese Wege, galaktisch,
o diese Stunde, die uns
die Nächte herüberwog in
die Last unsrer Namen. Es ist,
ich weiß es, nicht wahr,
daß wir lebten, es ging
blind nur ein Atem zwischen
Dort und Nicht-da und Zuweilen,
kometenhaft schwirrte ein Aug
auf Erloschenes zu, in den Schluchten,
da, wo's verglühte, stand
zitzenprächtig die Zeit,
an der schon empor- und hinab-
und hinwegwuchs, was
ist oder war oder sein wird — ,

ich weiß,
ich weiß und du weißt, wir wußten,
wir wußten nicht, wir
waren ja da und nicht dort,
und zuweilen, wenn
nur das Nichts zwischen uns stand, fanden
wir ganz zueinander.[7]

[7]   SO MANY CONSTELLATIONS that
are held out to us. I was,
when I looked at you — when? —
outside by
the other worlds.

O these ways, galactic.
O this hour, that weighed
nights over for us into
the bruden of our names. It is
I know, not true
that we lived, there moved,
blindly, no more than a beath between
there and not-there, and at times
our eyes whirred comet-like
towards things extinguished, in chasm,
and where they had burnt out,
splendid with teats, stood Time
on which already grew up
and down and away all that
is or was or will be — .

The opening sentence — "Soviel Gestirne, die man uns hinhält" — embodies the irreducible tension of the poem, the tension between "man" and "uns," pronouns appearing here side-by-side with nothing in-between but a single space, a brief void. "Man" is the agent of the action described, but who is this "man"? More generic even than the American "man," the German "man" signifies a faceless one among the many. Who and how much might Celan mean by "uns"?

If readers could establish a one-to-one correspondence between a pronoun and *its* referent — between a signifier and *its* signified, between a name and *its* named — then they could "solve" the poem (or watch it collapse onto *itself*). But Celan sustains unsolvability in order to traverse ways in which the relationship between language and living is unsolvable and irreducible.

> Ich war,
> als ich dich ansah — wann? — ,
> draußen bei
> den andern Welten.

Outside by the other worlds, worlds other than those of naming and the language manœuvers which naming sponsors. The previous "uns" now splits into "ich" and "dich" (the accusative "du") in a manner suggestive of originary designations — as if, through this poem, we witness again and always the first act of differential naming. "Uns," in this setting, does not suggest difference. Here "uns" is holistic, but "ich" and "du" already exclusive. Could the "wann?" be wondering about the state of this space before the time we were differentiated by our names?

> O diese Wege, galaktisch,
> o diese Stunde, die uns
> die Nächte herüberwog in
> die Last unsrer Namen.

Who is the agent of these galactic ways? Who named the duration an hour and so split eternity into increments? Is time itself the agent that shattered a previously undifferentiated us into the scattered ones burdened with separate names?

> Es ist,
> ich weiß es, nicht wahr,

> I know.
> I know and you know, we knew,
> we did not know, we
> were there, after all, and not there
> and at times when
> only the void stood between us we got
> all, the way to each other.   (translation by Michael Hamburger)

daß wir lebten, es ging
blind nur ein Atem zwischen
Dort and Nicht-da and Zuweilen,
kometenhaft schwirrte ein Aug
auf Erloschenes zu, in den Schluchten,
da, wo's verglühte, stand
zitzenprächtig die Zeit,
an der schon empor- und hinab-
und hinwegwuchs, was
ist oder war oder sein wird — ,

"Es ist ... es ging," these two cosmic its, refer at once to nothing and to everything. "I know" is in the present tense, this time of differentiation in name. But "I know" too that "we lived," in the past — a past prior to the inception of naming when undifferentiated-usness was the essential condition of beings. In these lines references to time and to space are given the respect accorded proper names, the respect of capitalization — "*Dort,*" "*Nicht-da,*" "*Zuweilen*" — suggesting unitary time and space, without rigid demarcations and the referential world such boundaries bring about.

ich weiß,
ich weiß und du weißt, wir wußten,
wir wußten nicht, wir
waren ja da und nicht dort,

"I" and "you" now know. But once "we knew" something else, or rather we did not know anything at all, in the same way that we now know knowing and so seed knowing in names. What was it that we knew? We "were there" but also "not there" — not there in the sense of the presence experienced by one who addresses or is addressed in name. "Dort," "nicht," and "zuweilen" are no longer capitalized because now they have been abstracted in graduated names.

und zuweilen, wenn
nur das Nichts zwischen uns stand, fanden
wir ganz zueinander.

No names between us, separating us, differentiating us. Only the void, the "Nichts," the namelessness, when we were us and could be so completely unalone, before naming turned us into separate barges carrying individual cargo.

"Das Nichts" will resound in another poem in the collection, "Psalm," in which the Thou the poem seeks may be a Creator willing to carry the weight of the name — even if it be "Niemand" — rather than demanding we bear it. A Creator who will not insist on splitting "wir" into "ich" and "du":

Gelobt seist du, Niemand.
Dir zulieb wollen

wir blühn.
Dir
entgegen.

Ein Nichts
waren wir, sind wir, werden
wir bleiben, blühend:
die Nichts-, die
Niemandsrose.[8]

The *burden* of our names is the matter here, but one could also turn to Celan's work to aid a discussion of the boon of our names. For instance, the case could be made that Celan bitterly resented the anonymity with which the Holocaust Jews went to their deaths. Could that SS man have carried out his "duty" had he beseeched each victim-in-waiting, "Tell me, please, your name. Has it served you well? Would you have chosen it had it not been chosen for you?" The ashes of the nameless drift. Clearly Celan's poetry bespeaks a reverence for calling "things" by their proper and precise names.

Several Celan poems appear to be about neither the burden of our names, nor a reverence for names, but the very impossibility of naming: "Sprachgitter," "Kiesel in Mund," "Siberisch," "Die silbe Schmerz," "Nacht," .... Yet Celan's poetry does provoke and sustain several questions: What is the relationship among God, Language, Man, and Nature and how is naming implicated? What was "it" like before naming? And at whose behest did we originally name and continue to name? God's? Language's? Man's? Nature's? Who/What is the agent? Which may be to ask, Who/What is to blame for this nominal bind we find ourselves in?

Four years before Paul Celan was born, Walter Benjamin cultivated these questions in "On Language as Such and on the Language of Man." In this essay, Benjamin's language philosophy suggests the Chassidic entrapment and release of

---

[8]   Praised be your name, no one.
For your sake
we shall flower.
Towards you.

A nothing
we were, are, shall
remain, flowering;
the nothing —, the
no one's rose.

(translation by Michael Hamburger)

the divine spark (the Shekinah) from matter.[9] He holds that every event and thing in nature — animate or inaminate — in some way participates in language, because it is "the nature of all to communicate their mental meanings."[10] The crux, claims Benjamin, is that this communication is guaranteed by God through the human language act of naming.

"On Language" misleads while leading: Benjamin's essaying is often as ambiguous and exacting as Celan's poetry, prompting Martin Jay to exclaim that the "unique texture" and "studied intricacy" of his work defy translation or reduction. Moreover, continues Jay, Benjamin's "mode of reasoning was rarely inductive or deductive, a reflection of [his] insistence that every sentence must be mediated through the totality of the essay in order to be understood fully."[11] Not formally logical, this mode of reasoning can be characterized as permutational, a telling example of which occurs early in "On Language" as Benjamin attempts to stipulate definitions of key terms:

> Mental being communicates itself in, not through, a language, which means: it is not outwardly identical with linguistic being. Mental is identical with linguistic being only insofar as it is capable of communication. What is communicable in a mental entity is its linguistic entity. Language therefore communicates the particular linguistic being of things, but their mental being only insofar as this is directly included in their linguistic being, insofar as it is capable of being communicated.[12]

Benjamin's principle of progression apparently entails his reaching right back into the text he has just presented to grasp, twist, then pull forward a new sentence. At any given moment, this involved approach sustains many layers of meaning and suggests many levels of interpretation without ever providing for — even by text's end — a one, single, comprehensive interpretation.[13] Rather than being simply and annoyingly contradictory, Benjamin's discourse appears dialectical in

---

[9] According to Chassidic thought, God made the universe out of Himself; thus the God-Spirit is in every piece of matter. The pious person, approaching the object in a pious manner, releases the divine spark. (See especially Martin Buber's writings on the subject.)

[10] Walter Benjamin, "On Language as Such and on the Language of Man," transl. by Edmund Jephcott, in: *Reflections*, edited with an introduction by Peter Demetz, (New York: Schocken, 1986), p. 314.

[11] Martin Jay, *The Dialectical Imagination*, (Boston: Little, Brown and Company, 1973), p. 175.

[12] Op. cit., p. 316.

[13] In his *Moscow Diary*, (Cambridge, Massachusetts: Harvard University Press, 1986) Benjamin complains that "in Germany the only thing demanded [of the writer] is results. No one cares to know how you have arrived at them" (12). Perhaps Benjamin's own rhetoric is a response to this condition.

a manner idiosyncratic and deeply characteristic of his work. This manner practically requires that his commentators follow suit (but, unlike Benjamin, commentators feel compelled to indicate sharp turns in explanation with markers such as "yet," "on the other hand," "paradoxically," "ironically," and, of course, "curiously.") We grant the poet open-endedness but complain that Benjamin, as essayist — as teacher, guide, and clarifier — raises many more expectations than he fulfills, often forgetting his repeated assertion that systematic thought and language manipulates names in a way that always brings about brutality.

In his biography of lifelong friend Benjamin, Jewish theologian and mystic Gershom Scholem remembers that the essay "On Language" began in letters between the two at a time when Benjamin was interested in mathematics. "He handed me a copy in December 1916 upon his return to Berlin," recalls Scholem, "designating it as the first part, to be followed by two more."[14] The essay did not reach a large audience until 1955 — fifteen years after the almost-forgotten author's death — when Theodor Adorno succeeded in winning over the Suhrkamp Verlag for the publication of a two-volume edition of Benjamin's writings. Still, it is significant to remember that the essay is early Benjamin, indicative of a metaphysical language philosophy which he never abandoned, one which pre-supposes "language as an ultimate reality, perceptible only in its manifestation, inexplicable and mystical"[15] — a position much irritating to his later Marxist colleagues.[16]

Benjamin evidences the arguments of "On Language" with a reading of Genesis I, defensively adding that his aim is "neither biblical interpretation, nor subjection of the Bible to objective consideration as revealed truth,"[17] but exegesis of the biblical text regarding the nature and origin of language. "The Bible," explains Benjamin, "in regarding itself as a revelation, must necessarily evolve the fundamental linguistic facts."[18] Benjamin, however, is hardly convincing; at the

---

[14] Gershom Sholem, *Walter Benjamin : The Story of a Friendship*, (Philadelphia: The Jewish Publication Society of America, 1981), p. 34.

[15] Op. cit., p. 322.

[16] Eugene Lunn, *Marxism and Modernism*, (Berkeley: University of California, 1982), p. 18). In the Introduction to *Illuminations*, a selection of Benjamin's work chosen and introduced by Hannah Arendt, she writes: "What strikes one as indecision in his [Benjamin's] letters, as though he were vacillating between Zionism and Marxism, in truth was probably due to the bitter insight that all solutions were not only objectively false and inappropriate to reality, but would lead him personally to false salvation, no matter whether that salvation was labelled Moscow or Jerusalem." Hannah Arendt, *Illuminations. Essays and Reflections of Walter Benjamin*, transl. by Harry Zohn, (New York: Harcourt, Brace & World, 1968), p. 36.

[17] Op. cit., p. 322.

[18] Ibidem.

core of his theory of language is the belief that the world was created by the word of God.[19]

Benjamin makes (in Peter Demetz' words) "a halfhearted attempt" at reconciling the two creation stories of the Old Testament (xxii-xxiii), before embracing the narrative of Genesis I. He urges agreement that the recurrent rhythm of "Let there be/He made (created)/He named" indicates a

> deep and clear relation of [God's] creative act to language ... . With the creative omnipotence of language [the relation] begins, and at the end language as it were assimilates the created, names it. Language is therefore both creative and the finished creation, it is word and name.[20]

The pure relation of name to knowledge lives only in God; in God, name is the pure medium of knowledge because it is "inwardly identical with the creative word."[21] Man's blessing and burden reside in reflecting God's absolute and creative word in "names." Of course, human language can but mirror the divine word in name. Thus, claims Benjamin, human language will remain always "limited and analytical" with respect to the "absolutely unlimited and creative infinity of the divine word."[22]

The names man gives to and receives from others may merely reflect the divine word, but name giving maintains man's closeness to God's creative energies, defining his particular mode of being and position in the cosmic order (Demetz xxiii). God empowers man to name; humans communicate themselves to God through name and in turn name nature according to the communication they receive from it — Benjamin's complex sense of "translation," and one infused with Chassidic mysticism. "God's creation," reminds Benjamin, "is completed [only] when things receive their names from man, from whom in name language alone speaks."[23]

Benjamin emphasizes that his (Chassidic and Romantic) language philosophy leaves inconceivable the "bourgeois" view of language as mere convention in which the word bears only an accidental, conventional relationship to its object. Just as inconceivable is the "mystical" view that the word embodies the essence of its object. This view is incorrect, Benjamin remarks, because "the thing in itself has no word, being created from God's word and known in its name by a human word."[24]

---

[19] Cf. Martin Jay, *The Dialectical Imagination*, op. cit., p. 261.

[20] Op. cit., p. 322–323.

[21] Ibidem.

[22] Ibidem.

[23] Op. cit., p. 319.

[24] Op. cit., p. 324.

Language, then, far from a mere means of convention, is instead to Benjamin's mind a medium of being. In his system, all creation participates in an infinite process of communication, communion, continuum among God, Language, Man, and Nature — a dialogue sponsored and guaranteed by the naming act.

Benjamin's declaration that "in name appears the essential law of language, according to which to express oneself and to address everything else amounts to the same"[25] reveals a belief in the dialogic nature of naming, a belief Celan (as we have seen) echoes in his "Meridian" speech and demonstrates in his poetics. Nevertheless, Celan would not have contended as readily as Benjamin that communion in language occurs or is guaranteed by God. One reading "Psalm," for instance, finds "a natural God-seeker who has failed to find God, yet cannot leave off calling into nothingness and emptiness in the hope of an answer."[26] Other Celan poems apparently also question God's existence, or at least God's continuing intervention in human affairs. Consider, for example, "Du Sei Wie Du," a poem Celan wrote in 1969 shortly before his suicide, in the time between the Israeli/Egyptian Six-Day War and his journey to Palestine:

> DU SEI WIE DU, immer
>
> "Stant vp Jherosalem inde
> erheyff dich"
>
> Auch wer das Band zerschnitt zu dir hin ... .[27]

"The very one who slashed the bond unto you ... ." Meditating on his own translation of the Celan line, Felstiner reminds that in Jewish history sinful people, not their God, broke the mutual covenant. "Yet now," Felstiner reflects, "if he [Celan], like Isaiah, speaks to the Jewish dead and to a people returning from exile, then the very one who slashed the bond ... may also be God."[28]

Late in "On Language" Benjamin dampens his earlier enthusiasm for the dialogic, communal potential of the naming act, chronicling the human's loss of

---

[25] Op. cit., 319.

[26] Siegbert Prawer, "Paul Celan," in: *Essays on Contemporary German Literature*, ed. by Brian Keith-Smith, V. 4, (London: Wolff, 1969), p. 177.

[27]   YOU BE LIKE YOU, ever.

Ryse vp Ierosalem and
rowse thyselfe

The very one who slashed the bond unto you.

(translation by John Felstiner).

[28] John Felstiner, "Paul Celan in Translation: 'Du sei wie Du'," in *Studies in Twentieth Century Literature*, (Fall 1983), V. 8, N. 1, pp. 95–96.

paradise as the price paid for abusing the privilege of naming. The life of man in pure language-mind was "blissful," chimes Benjamin, but then man was seduced fatefully by the knowledge of good and evil:

> Knowledge of good and evil abandons name, it is a knowledge from outside, the uncreated imitation of the creative word. Name steps outside itself in this knowledge: the Fall marks the birth of the *human word*, in which name no longer lives intact.[29]

God created language to commune with His creations and His creations with each other, Benjamin proposes, but then man reached outside the bond, seeking a knowledge outside of name, incurring the Fall. As consequence of the Fall of language-mind, he adds, the word could no longer communicate itself but had to communicate something other than itself. Moreover, once fallen, man indulged in naming and so began overnaming, resulting in abstractions, generalizations, and the formal logic which separates the paradisiac language of man from its lapsed complement.

If we consider the Thou sought by many of Celan's poems to be Language itself — a language, as earlier suggested, lost but not forgotten — could this language be the "paradisiac language of man" which Benjamin considers "one of perfect knowledge"? That is, the paradisiac language, the perfect knowledge which preceded the inception of the human word, the human name? When word and knowledge were one and a word could communicate itself instead of only something *other* than itself? A language not of "ich" and "du" but of "uns"?

In the midst of squinting differences and intriguing similarities, the preoccupations with the naming act of Celan and Benjamin find this significant convergence: Both writers posit the onetime existence of an *Ursprache* — a paradisiacal and pristine language, a lost language indicative of our lost innocence. Moreover, both urge the possibility of recovery — or, more precisely, redemption — of this lost language. For instance, in "Schwarz," from *Atemwende*, the "du" Celan addresses appears to be the remnants and relics of a lost language still perceived, but ever so faintly:

> SCHWARZ,
> wie die Erinnerungswunde,
> wühlen die Augen nach dir
> in dem von Herzzahnen hell-
> gebissenen Kronland,
> das unser Bett bleibt:
>
> durch diesen Schacht mußt du kommen —
> du kommst ... .

---

[29] Op. cit., p. 327.

Das Namengeben hat ein Ende,
über dich werf ich mein Schicksal.[30]

If we are to be whole again, the lost language "must come" through the slender shaft of possibility opened by the act of writing poetry.

What is the role of the poet in such a project? A number of Celan poems feature geological vocabulary, often suggesting that the poet is a miner of sorts, struggling to recover artifacts of language from the past. James Lyon notices that in Celan's poetry

> Word clusters dealing with stone serve a function for the poet similar to the usefulness of stones for geologists. They are a tie to that which has been lost, forgotten, or silenced. In their muteness, the rocks of the earth store up a living record which testifies to more pristine forms of existence. In the case of the poet it is existence of words. Celan's internal landscape — an ontological location of poetic creativity not to be confused with the external world of sight and sound — sometimes uses ore-bearing rock to designate such petrified pristine language forms[.][31]

Lyon then exhibits "Erzflitter," from the late collection *Schneepart*:

Erzflitter, tief im
Aufruhr, Erzväter.

Du behilfst dir
damit,
als sprächen mit ihnen
Angiospermen
ein offenes
Wort.

Kalkspur Posaune.

---

[30]   BLACK
as the memory's wound
the eyes thrash after you
through the dominion, flashbitten by heart-teeth,
that remains of our bed:

through this shaft you must come —
you do come ... .
Namegiving comes to an end,
over you I cast my fate.   (translation by Christiane Staninger and Dale Gowen)

[31] James Lyons, "Paul Celan's Language of Stone: The Geology of the Poetic Landscape," in *Colloquia Germanica* (1974), V.3-4, n.2, p. 302.

Verlorenes findet
in den Karstwannen
Kargheit, Klarheit.[32]

Lyon finds much of Celan's poetry actively resisting the prattle and redundancy of modern speech "by recovering speech particles that have been lost or forgotten and allowing them to return to a condition of pristine vitality."[33]

Like Celan, Benjamin takes "the intention of [his] investigations" to be "to plumb the depths of language and thought ... by drilling rather than excavating."[34] Hannah Arendt espies this intention throughout Benjamin's literary studies — irrespective of his current leanings — the intention

> not to investigate the utilitarian or communicative functions of linguistic creations, but to understand them in their crystallized and thus ultimately fragmentary form as intentionless and non-communicative utterances of a "world essence."[35]

What else does this mean, asks Arendt, than that he understood language as an essentially poetic phenomenon, the decayed aspects of which "survive in new crystallized forms and shapes ... — as 'thought fragments,' as something 'rich and strange,' and perhaps even as everlasting *Urphänomene*."[36]

Das Namengeben hat ein Ende,
über dich werf ich mein Schicksal.[37]

---

[32] ARCHTAWDRY, in full
riot, patriarchs.

You quite get by,
as though
angiosperms
took you
in confidence.

Chalkline trumpets.

Lost item find
in the lime troughs
scarcity, clarity.   (translation by Dale Gowen)

[33] Op. cit., p. 314.

[34] *Briefe,* I, p. 329.

[35] Hannah Arendt, *Illuminations*, op. cit., p. 50.

[36] Ibidem, p. 51.

[37] Ibidem.

Where the name-giving ends, the lost language begins again. (But what is the "fate" of the poet at such a time?)

Drilling for this lost language, Celan privileges praxis, Benjamin theory. And so Benjamin closes "On Language" with an evocation and explanation of the loss as well as an implicit suggestion that community thrives most where there is no naming:

> There is, in the relation of human languages to that of things, something that can be approximately described as "over-naming": over-naming as the deepest linguistic reason for all melancholy and (from the point of view of the thing) of all deliberate muteness. Over-naming as the linguistic being of melancholy points to another curious relation of language: the overprecision that obtains in the tragic relationship between the languages of human speakers.
>
> [I]t is very conceivable that ... we find [in] a translation of the language of things an infinitely higher language ... . We are concerned here with nameless, nonacoustic languages, languages issuing from matter; here we should recall the material community of things in their communication.
>
> Moreover, the communication of things is certainly communal in a way that grasps the world as such as an undivided whole.[38]

Benjamin's directive to "recall the material community of things" resonates with Celan's predilection for addressing concrete matter as "Thou" (as in, for example, "Du Baum"). Such gesture by Celan suggests his sharing Benjamin's dream to put back together a world that was once an "undivided whole" by bringing back together matter and language.

This search for an *Ursprache* unsullied by the divisions drawn by human over-namings would be seen by some language philosophers — such as the deconstructionists — as an already nostalgic, delusory quest for origins. The deconstructionists flatly refute that a pure language, or even a human language capable of conjuring presence, ever existed. Seen in this light, Celan's and Benjamin's projects fall prey to the "ruse of reference," a critique made famous by French philosopher/critic Jacques Derrida. The ruse of reference, Derrida proffers, follows from the primordial human longing for a return to origins, for a retreat from history back to paradise. The path of consciousness, thought, and linguistic development, which sets the boundaries of man's historical existence, moves always in a straight line. However, observes Derrida, the nostalgic lure of preconsciousness — the seduction of innocence — is "inscribed in *circular* characters." Language and interpretation, like the movement of reflection, are deflected toward their own absent beginnings. Adds theologian Carl Raschke,

---

[38] Op. cit., p. 327–330.

The search for the Rosetta stone of reference in modern poetics and semiotics is a chapter in what Derrida regards as the "idealistic" bewitchment of thought, the impulse to leap into the magic circle of a self-enfolding discourse and dance the hypnotic rondo of "verification" and "certitude."[39]

Nevertheless, the promise of a pristine language remained crucial to the thought and language of Celan and Benjamin, of a supreme importance surely influenced by their personal histories as Jews in a time of horrific overprecision in the lexicons of humans ... and thus between the humans themselves.

Celan's poetry is thick with the smoke of the response of Central Europe in the Forties to a Jewish surname: "dein aschenes Haar Sulamith ... ."[40] Paul Celan's original name, of course, was Paul Ancel. Katharine Washburn and Margret Guillemin help to explain Celan's reasons for this reversal of syllables and its implications:

> After the war, orphaned by the German occupation and dispossessed by the Soviets, the survivor left Bucharest in 1947 with a rucksack of poems. Following a six-month sojourn in Vienna, he emigrated to Paris where he lived for a quarter of a century "after the first death" as Paul Celan.
>
> The pseudonym, contrived in Bucharest, and sealed in Vienna, from an anagram of the original name, dissolved its ambiguous cultural identity into a number of allusions to the primary concerns of his poetry [...] . We are accustomed, in the poems, to Celan's habit of breaking down a given word, exhausting it etymologically and supplying it with the densest and widest repertoire of associations. In the name itself, we have the writer's shortest poem, composed at the edge of known languages.[41]

While never formally altering his name, Benjamin's affection for anagrams accompanied him throughout his life: In several of his essays he used the anagram Anni M. Bie instead of the name Benjamin.[42] And found in a notebook of Benjamin's writings from 1933 is a quizzical little piece titled "Agesilaus Santander," the opening to which reveals his recognition of the vulnerability brought upon him by his name:

---

[39] Carl Raschke, *Deconstruction and Theology*, (New York: Crossroad, 1982), p. 10–11.

[40] "your ashen hair, Sulamith," from "Todesfuge."

[41] Paul Celan, *Poems*, translated by Katharine Washburn and Margaret Guillemin, (San Francisco: North Point, 1986), p. vii–viii.

[42] Gershom Sholem, "Walter Benjamin and His Angels," in *On Jews and Judaism in Crisis*, ed. and translated by Werner J. Dannhauser, (New York: Schocken, 1976), p. 215.

When I was born the thought came to my parents that I might perhaps become a writer. Then it would be good if not everybody noticed at once that I was a Jew. That is why besides the name I was called they added two further, exceptional ones, from which one could see neither that a Jew bore them nor that they belonged to him as first names. Forty years ago no parental couple could prove itself more far-seeing. What it held to be only a remote possibility has come true.[43]

Seven years later, Benjamin killed himself on the border between France and Spain in fear of being dragged back to what had come true. In flight from the Nazis, he had crossed the Pyrenees into Spain with fellow refugees, when the local official at Port-Bou threatened to turn them back and extradite them to France. (Later the official shrugged that his was an idle threat, a bid for graft.) Who or What do we bring to account for the atrocities which have been committed in name and because of names? Is it that language as a bestowment giveth and taketh away?

But Benjamin, as one comes to expect, is as ambiguous as Celan on this matter. Numerous passages in "On Language" grant primacy to language, projecting language — as Celan often does — as an almost independent agent. Language, Benjamin explains at one point, "assimilates" the created by naming it, a phrase suggesting that language, not man, is agent of the naming act. In a similar casting, Benjamin posits that "[God] did not wish to subject [man] to language, but in man God set language, which had served *Him* as medium of creation, free. God rested when he had left his creative power to itself in man".[44] To *itself*? Is Benjamin implying that language has a life of its own and that God could repose only once He found host bodies for this uncontrollable potential? Language, flexing its very reflexivity across the affairs of man while God rests? Certainly Benjamin contends that the naming act conjoins the human and God, but he does not claim that God ever reentered human history to intervene in human language practice … . God? Language? Man? Nature? Clear only is that the naming act allows an I to conjure an Other, but also to contest, to conflict, and even to control that Other.

[43] Ibidem, p. 206.

[44] Walter Benjamin, "On Language as Such and on the Language of Man," translated by Edmund Jephcott, in *Reflections*, ed. with an introduction by Peter Demetz, (New York: Schocken, 1986), p. 323.

Stanley Corngold

Paul de Man's Confessional Anarchy

IN THE DISCUSSION PROVOKED by the publication of Paul de Man's wartime journalism, not all the appropriate lines of thought on autobiography and confession have been drawn. In these pages I want to explore the possibility of a substantial and informative connection between de Man's life and work — between his life, which now seems, for at least one important period (the years in Belgium in 1940-1943) to have been passionate, opportunistic, and blind — and his critical work, on the surface uncommitted, "rigorous" (as it is said), and lucid. The connections between the life and the work which emerge are ones of violence, the masking of violence, self-exculpation, provocation, and the repudiation of so-called lived experience. These connections inform the relation between de Man's literary criticism and his personal and political life; between de Man's criticism and the authors he reads; and between de Man's criticism and the readers whom he trained.

My task, then, is to build analogies and continuities between de Man's life and work. If my purpose could be solidly carried through, it would amount to the biography of his critical work — on the model, say, with all due adjustment of scale, of Joseph Frank's biography of the intellectual life of Dostoevskij. Within this project, de Man's writing would be seen, more or less plainly, as involuntary autobiography. This project seems do-able to some extent, because there now appears to be a considerable number of sentences in de Man's critical writings, which, in the light of his wartime experience, look as if they were boxed around by red crayon and cry out with autobiographical import; they can hardly be read otherwise.

Here is a striking example. First, the life. In a letter from Harvard days, written in January 1955, de Man informed Renato Poggioli that the anonymous denunciation accusing him of collaboration was a slander perpetrated by enemies of Hendrik de Man.[1] Hendrik de Man, the former Socialist minister condemned for collaborating with the Nazi occupiers, was Paul de Man's *uncle*; but in the apology which de Man wrote, de Man said he was his *father*.

---

[1] *Responses: On Paul de Man's Wartime Journalism*, ed. Werner Hamacher, Neil Hertz, and Thomas Keenan, (Lincoln and London: University of Nebraska Press, 1989), p. 475–477.

We have here what seems to be an intentional denial of paternity for the sake of political advantage and psychological gratification (a sort of defiance and provocation to future historians, very likely involving the exhilarating release from the constraints of empirical identity). And indeed, it worked: Harvard authorities appear to have taken de Man out from under suspicion, since he would presumably have already suffered enough from the sins visited on him by his "father."

To this biographical narrative, I now join the passage from de Man's critical essay, in *Allegories of Reading*, on Rousseau's *Confessions* — certainly his wildest piece: it is called "The Purloined Ribbon."[2] De Man writes, "With the threatening loss of control [of the meaning of a text], the possibility arises of the entirely gratuitous and irresponsible text, not just ... as an intentional denial of paternity for the sake of self-protection, but as the radical annihilation of the metaphor of selfhood and of the will."[3]

The passage recommends a kind of reading (gratuitous and irresponsible and sceptical of metaphors of selfhood) at the moment when our resistance to such reading is strongest. For here it is precisely no longer the case that this passage could persuasively say, "Do *not* read literature autobiographically." Instead, the passage insists on being read autobiographically. It says that de Man wished that his own life-stories and critical assertions, like Rousseau's, could amount to something quite different from an intentional denial of paternity for the sake of self-protection. De Man wants it to be true that his texts, too, spring from the entire dissolution of the individual personality and intensify that dissolution — producing for him a sort of allegorical existence, a life lived, like Thomas Mann's Felix Krull, *im Gleichnis*, figuratively only.

Here, now, is a second example of an autobiographical moment. We should imagine the burden of anxiety which de Man's past must have laid on him. At the outset of *Blindness and Insight*, de Man writes about "genuine" writers: "Considerations of the actual and historical existence of writers are a waste of time from a critical viewpoint. These regressive stages can only reveal an emptiness of which the writer himself is well aware when he begins to write".[4] This is de

---

[2] In *Modern Language Notes* 106 (December 1991): 1048–1051 Robert Ellrich discusses the fact, long identified in academic conversation, that the sentence from Rousseau's *Confessions* which de Man develops in this essay is not a sentence Rousseau ever wrote. De Man has Rousseau say the very opposite of what Rousseau said — and meant. The distortion was interpreted in a way protective of de Man by Ortwin de Graef, in "Silence to be Observed: A Trial for Paul de Man's Inexcusable Confessions," in: *(Dis)continuities: Essays on Paul de Man*, ed. Luc Herman, Kris Humbeeck, and Gert Lernout, (Amsterdam: Rodopi, 1989), p. 51–73.

[3] Paul de Man, *Allegories of Reading: Figural Language in Rousseau, Nietzsche, Rilke, and Proust*, (New Haven: Yale University Press, 1979), p. 296.

[4] Paul de Man, *Blindness and Insight: Essays in the Rhetoric of Contemporary Criticism*, 2nd ed. rev., (Minneapolis: University of Minnesota Press, 1983), p. 35.

Man's basic position, I believe, and can be summed up as the thesis of the "contingency of the empirical intention." It is the view that the divergence between the empirical personality and the project of constituting a work of thought or art is the "meaning" of that work. I stress a certain controlled and non-violent character to this divergence, conveyed by the sober tone of de Man's account. The divergence is induced by "an emptiness of which the writer is well aware."[5]

The thesis cannot but be read as self-serving: de Man's mature criticism would, for one thing, serve to protect his youthful journalism from the consequences of a too literal reading. It would prevent Nazistic, collaborationist, and anti-Semitic passages from being treated as the immediate reproduction of his personal intentions, desires, and beliefs. De Man's theoretical essays would have succeeded, in his own phrase, in "hid[ing] their self-obsessions behind a language of conceptual generality".[6]

This can be put more particularly. De Man, I believe, felt especially entitled to write about literature because, to an extreme degree, he had cast off ties to father — and also to wife, children, country, class, and political party — an experience of dispossession that he went on courting while in the United States, as he married bigamously, declared his uncle to be his father, and lied about his conduct during the war. It is as if each of these divestments of reality only increased the power of his investment in a certain impersonal conception of literature and criticism — an impersonality the degree of whose strictness in fact kept pace with the degree to which personal and worldly dispossession actually mattered to him.[7] But, it appears, he was unable to conceal in his works the traces of the things he renounced; in the end they reveal his anxiety that some of these renunciations might be viewed as having been made for personal advantage.

What bearing, then, on de Man's intellectual authority does his own claim have that to attend to "the actual and historical existence of writers" is "a waste of time from a critical viewpoint?" Because such a sentence, being autobiographical, interrupts and disturbs the surface-logic of his texts, I speak of "confessional anarchy." The confessional moment introduces a sort of violence into the exposition: it breaks up the order of the analysis — of Rousseau or of Serge Dubrovsky (whose celebration of the abundance of sensory perception in literature prompted

---

[5] Many passages in *Blindness and Insight* help make more explicit de Man's thesis of "the contingency [for literature] of the empirical intention," especially pp. 17, 34–35, and 41. These pages show that the condition of the apprehension of allegory, i.e. literature, is the obliteration of the personality, which in de Man's case meant importantly the political personality that he had particular reasons to obliterate.

[6] Paul de Man, *Allegories of Reading*, op. cit., p. 138.

[7] It would have been less a stake at Yale in the 1970s when, with de Man's personal and institutional power, the category of the referent made a marked comeback into his theories of reading.

de Man's turn against the "actual and historical existence of writers"). The sequence of disruptive, confessional moments in de Man's theoretical essays points back to another intention and composes another text for the reader — a text of suspicion, of consternation with respect to the authority of the ruling argument. De Man's sentences have not sufficiently left behind the interests of the empirical personality: they could intend to be self-serving.

The divergence between empirical and theoretical selves is supposed to be a rigorous matter: it is an affair of law, of ascetic discipline. Its proper outcome is that literature comes to possess an authority which the language "of the everyday" does not; for with respect to the language of the everyday, speakers are always free to maintain that their language does not express their intentions and desires. More radically still, the everyday speaker, says de Man, "is always free to make what he wants differ from what he says he wants." The autobiographical intention that surfaces in the midst of literary theory, however, introduces another kind of turbulence — the turbulence of incomplete "separation" or "divergence." Here the interests of the empirical ego irrupt into the systematic semiotic surface of the text: the effect is hybrid, anarchic. The work of theoretical reflection is supposed to signal, after all, "its separation from empirical reality, its divergence, as a sign, from a meaning that depends for its existence on the constitutive activity of this sign." Now the work signals only that another meaning is in play, one about which it cannot even be serenely said that it "depends for its existence on the constitutive activity of the sign." For, when intents are "empirical," the writer is "always free" to impose on the meaning of the sign the meaning of what "he says he wants."[8] What the said sign produces is only an illusion.

We would appear to have arrived at a difficult knot in the project that aimed to recover an autobiographical subject from de Man's theoretical writing. We have not encountered shaped life: we encounter intellectual violence instead. At particular moments, with particular transparency, the author allows his work to perform its own destruction. In the instant of defining, in the language of literary theory, the essence of literature as an ascesis of the empirical ego, he stains the theoretical statement with an assertion of ego. This is to produce turbulence of such density, and spread suspicion so widely, that the goal of finite autobiographical recovery (of the views, desires, and intentions of the person de Man) is obfuscated. For if, in moments of such transparency, de Man offers his empirical self to be seized, as what can it be seized, other than the will to turbulence? The confessional moment now appears to be essentially a moment of defiance and provocation to future historians; or — in another focus — an irrepressible and opaque symptom of an unmastered past.

---

[8] Paul de Man, *Blindness and Insight*, op. cit., p. 11.

The latter focus is provided by the Mitscherlichs, the theorists of mourning. De Man, refusing to be an "invalid," remains unable to mourn; for "only the invalid," they write,

> whose suffering from symptoms is greater than the profit of repression, is ready to loosen the censor of his consciousness for the return of what has been denied and forgotten [...] . What, under censorship of our consciousness in place for more than two decades cannot be admitted as painful memories can return out of the past unasked for, unwanted, for it has not been "coped with," is not a past that one has laboured to understand.

In the end, "mourning can only be accomplished when we know what it is we must detach ourselves from ('wovon wir uns lösen müssen')."[9] If we do not know what it is we must detach ourselves from, that unknown is likely in moments of inattention to detach itself in a fragmentary and unruly manner. It is of course true that nowhere in de Man's writings does he explicitly identify the pro-Nazi, anti-Semitic articles of his youth. But the force of repression flickers at moments, admits shadowy signs of the thing repressed, and disturbs the theoretical analysis. Here is another example from *The Rhetoric of Romanticism*, where de Man is writing on Baudelaire's poetry. The "sheer blind *violence*" that Nietzsche allegedly associated with the "movement of an *army*" of tropes is "not just a power of *displacement*, be it understood as recollection or interiorization or any other *'transport'*."[10]

One could conceivably approach these moments of confessional violence from the opposite direction, one that would precisely stress de Man's knowingness. Through the turbulence of apparent confession, one could say, de Man deliberately means to exhibit the phenomenon of artistic divergence in its *in*completeness. He performs (according to this view of things) a struggle to fight free to an artistic transcendence that must not be motivated by empirical self-interest. But because the struggle is impossible to win, it is always fated to acknowledge self-interest. On this view, de Man would be confessing, well in advance, to the worst suspicions that could be harboured against him; he would be confessing even to crimes

---

[9] Alexander und Margarete Mitscherlich, *Die Unfähigkeit zu trauern*, (München: Piper, 1967) p. 24 and p. 82. [*The Inability to Mourn: Principles of Collective Behavior*, trans. Beverly Placzek, (New York: Grove Press, 1975)]. Discussed in Patricia Herminghouse, "Vergangenheit als Problem der Gegenwart: zur Darstellung des Faschismus in der neueren DDR-Literatur," in: *Literatur der DDR in den siebziger Jahren*, ed P.U. Hohendahl and Patricia Herminghouse, (Frankfurt: Suhrkamp, 1983), p. 270. A very rich conjunction of the work of the Mitscherlichs with that of de Man — suggesting the deconstructionist displacement of the charismatic object of mourning to the "always already" mortified referent-world of language itself — is found in Eric Santner, *Stranded Objects: Mourning, Memory, and Film in Postwar Germany* (Ithaca: Cornell University Press, 1990), pp 13–19.

[10] Paul de Man, *The Rhetoric of Romanticism*, (New York: Columbia University Press, 1984), p. 262. (emphasis added).

and involvements that he does not believe are his own, because such transcendence can never be realized; it is, in the best case, only a desideratum.

Forget that this thesis is implausible. Forget the unlikelihood that de Man's autobiographical intrusions are motivated by nothing more specific than the need to confess the guiltiness of the creature as such — markers of the transcendence only promised but not delivered by literature and theory. The result is still textual violence.

It is best now just plainly to acknowledge this factor, for which we could settle on the term "anarchy" — a turmoil in the identity of the autobiographical sign, its uncertain status between motivated and blurted, between exculpatory and contemplative, between helpless and defiant. It engenders a mood and scene of anarchy.

This violence, I shall now conclude, is the decisive element in de Man's autobiography. His real autobiography is not "literature" — not the orderly divergence of his empirical self-interests from his theoretical project — but, drastic as this may sound, the perpetuation of textual violence and anarchy.

This conclusion is so disturbing that I want to be very sure there is no way around it. But review the following argument:

1. If we have succeeded in identifying specific autobiographical confessional moments, then we note, too, that they violate the logic of the theoretical text.

2. But what if, despite their appearance as confessional moments, we have got the correspondences wrong — i.e. picked out moments when de Man is not in fact writing confessionally or else found for these moments the wrong empirical correlatives, so that, for example, the Rousseau's denial of paternity does not return to de Man's own denial of paternity for the sake of self-protection?

3. The result, then, *faute de mieux*, is that we are forced to suspect confessional turbulence and textual violence at other places in de Man's texts — indeed, in principle at every other place, because we cannot forget that we have been alerted to their existence.

De Man could want this surface of suspicion or not want it. But this surface appears, willy-nilly, to be a fact for the reader. The violence has been set in motion by the loose circulation in de Man's theoretical writing of the metonyms of an empirical subject.

I want to offer at this point a position on confessional anarchy in de Man. Since it is hard to believe that the autobiographical correspondences in de Man's remarks about paternity and about the irrelevance of the empirical life of authors (along with others remarks of this kind) are only random and meaningless, then it follows that there exist moments when de Man deliberately writes autobiography while pretending not to do so. A corollary: when passages appear not to have been informed by an autobiographical intent, we can assume that here de Man has decided not to write autobiography. But the distinction between such moments is not strict. According to Thomas Mann: "*not* to want to do something may be in the long run a mental content impossible to subsist on; between not willing a certain thing and not willing at all — in other words, yielding to another person's will, there may lie too small a space for the idea of freedom to squeeze into."[11] If this argument is right, then it may never have been enough for de Man not to want to confess his wartime experience; the outcome of this shrinkage of freedom was his yielding to "another person's will," which in every case could amount, of course, to one's own insistent public conscience.

The outcome of this point is that even places where de Man was determined not to write autobiography contain traces of the very thing he means to conceal — a fascination with power in time of war; and therefore de Man should be read autobiographically everywhere. (That de Man may have feared to excuse himself does not mean that he did not try.)[12] It is with respect to this half-conscious project of doing textual violence that readers can and indeed must read all his critical work.

A good deal of this textual violence is almost certainly a result of de Man's wartime experience. The anarchy in his critical writings appears to repeat and elaborate his experience of the war.

Several weeks after the Nazi deportation of Dutch Jews had begun, de Man published in Brussels an article encouraging the deportation of Jewish writers at the same time that he was rebuking the attitude of "vulgar" anti-Semites. More than a year later, he is still found attacking the "degenerate," "especially Jewish" Expressionist artists for their failure of "moral [or intellectual or spiritual] honesty," though he frames this slur with the oppositional gesture of praising the "peculiar" theses of German Expressionism. Nevertheless, underlying the occasional surface resistance of some of his pieces, his decision to work with the Occupation remains evident. From late 1942 on, after his successor on *Le Soir* was fingered and assassinated by the Resistance, de Man would have felt threatened by the violence of his collaboration. In the years following the Nazi defeat, this violence would have occupied him as the imagination of the coming defeat of his person and his career when his writings were exposed.

His mature work is organized on a model structurally identical with his collaborationist experience; it is one based on a primary violence with which the author is leagued even when he flinches from it. At times, within this scene, de Man occupies different positions, but one position remains dominant.

In the late work (1) the primary catastrophe of the German Occupation resurfaces as "the origin" of language or human society — a "power of death." (2) "Literary language," "poetic consciousness," "the text," come closest to reflecting this experience: they name the catastrophe and otherwise convey its

---

[11] Thomas Mann, "Mario and the Magician," in: *'Death in Venice' and Seven Other Stories*, trans. H.T. Lowe-Porter, (New York: Vintage, 1964), p. 173–74.

[12] De Graef, "Silence to be Observed," op. cit. See footnote 2, supra.

violence through their "relentless," "impersonal" dispersion of meaning. (3) The critic collaborates with this catastrophe as its interpreter, restating the truth of universal disruption. (4) He encourages readers to abandon any recourse to their empirical experience (vulgarly, their "knowledge of life") for help or understanding, since experience is in ruins.

To this extent the interpreter is in control of what he does. But this model leaves out the operations of a trauma — the incursion of an invading power, coercive, but offering the prospect of collaboration. If, however, you collaborate with an enemy resistingly, you will exhibit the distortions of stress; at the bursting point, you will be broken. The violence of the invading power has been internalized, redistributed, made random and unmanageable.

De Man was shattered in places by the operation of a force whose identity (Nazism in its manic, genocidal brutality) he mystified in the 1940s. Thereafter, he continued to mystify power, calling it "literature" — literature that always had to be more exigent than any ordinary instance of it (a single book or author or reading). The whole and surprising thrust of de Man's late view of literature is of an agency inhuman, mechanical, systematic, violent, and uncontainable. This power may be (mis)identified in his work; more important are the effects of violence it produces in his critical writings.

My thesis about the principal violence and hence unreliability of de Man's autobiographically-charged theory will finally come as no surprise to readers familiar with de Man, since this suspicion is in line with one that de Man himself explicitly puts forward. In his essay "Autobiography as De-facement," he asserts the impoverishing and disfiguring function of autobiography, separating the notion of autobiography as specifiable genre, which is indefensible, from "the autobiographical" as a mode of reading. Nothing in principle stands in the way of autobiographical reading anytime and any place.[13] That is one rule about autobiography in de Man, namely, that it is permitted. But keep in mind that it will not succeed, since it will not circumvent the rhetorical complications of its own leading figure — prosopopeia; this stricture is the second rule about autobiography. What once again emerges is that "it is not *a priori* certain that literature is a reliable source of information about anything but its own language."[14]

This second rule, therefore, makes autobiographical reading not finally persuasive at all: this point is developed in "Autobiography as De-facement," in which the autobiographical reader figures as policeman and autobiographical

---

[13] Though that would certainly involve the return, into the scene of interpretation, of the logocentric Gang of Five: perception, consciousness, intention, reference, and career.

[14] Paul de Man, *The Resistance of Theory*, (Minneapolis: University of Minnesota Press, 1986), p. 11.

writing and reading arise from a "defacement of the mind."[15] The same negative thrust is found in the earlier piece in *Allegories of Reading*, "Semiology and Rhetoric," first composed in 1973.[16] Here de Man addresses the only specious orderliness of the then current critical scene, where it is assumed that the formal dimensions of literary works are under control, well-policed, under the sway of "law and order." De Man is exploiting a parallel between essentialist linguistic structuralism and Agnew-like government on the grounds of their common resistance to theory and other subversive acts of thought. This atmosphere, de Man continues, has furthered a vulgar criticism sending out expeditions to referents: hence the current emphasis — he says — on "hybrid texts considered to be partly literary and partly referential, on popular fictions deliberately aimed towards social and psychological gratification, on literary autobiography as a key to the understanding of the self, and so on."[17]

This is the more nearly native strain: de Man is once again warning against autobiography, against the project of reading autobiographically, precisely because it introduces a false impression of order (in fact by a use of police power) into what must be the sole principle of order in reading — the technically-correct, deconstructive, rhetorical reading. The autobiographical reading, in the case of de Man's own work, would literally invite police intervention into the schoolroom, into the scene of the ascetically correct reading of de Man from within — would bring in school inspectors to actually disrupt more than the figure-dance of *Reading de Man Reading*. One scruple about this injunction against autobiography though.

If de Man warns against the vulgar gratifications of literary autobiography, how, in this light, should we understand those passages in his work about which there exists not the slightest doubt that they are autobiographical — that is, neither rigorously theoretical nor duplicitiously autobiographical but rigorously autobiographical? They are statements coming entirely under the generic head of autobiography — the foreword to the revised, second edition of *Blindness and Insight* and the preface to *The Rhetoric of Romanticism* — and they bear on the so-called "turn" in de Man's intellectual career. And it is just because de Man is speaking with the pragmatic authority of explicit autobiographical statement that what he says in this mode has dominated the readings made of him by friendly commenta-

---

[15] This is entirely opposite to what Rousseau explicitly says about the constructive power of the autobiographical imagination in the *Confessions*. For the *Confessions* are organized around Rousseau's claim that, by recovering the experience of spectacular intellectual power, he has proved the coherence of his moral personality. This recovery occurs as the content of a moment of *déjà vu*. See Stanley Corngold, *The Fate of the Self*, (New York: Columbia University Press, 1986), p. 223–225.

[16] *Diacritics* 3 (1973), p. 27–33.

[17] Paul de Man, *Allegories of Reading*, op. cit., p. 3.

tors. Christopher Norris's entire book on de Man, for example, subtitled *Deconstruction and the Critique of Aesthetic Ideology*, is organized around the interpretation of the turn as the turn to a type of politically-engaged activist criticism
aimed against a sinister "aesthetic ideology."[18] The same is true of Lindsay
Waters' introduction to his collection of de Man's scattered *Critical Writings —
1953-1978*. It is revealing that even friendly critics will read de Man autobiographically if this mode of reading helps support their belief that de Man's critical
power does indeed arise from the ascetic renunciation of easier modes of thinking
and writing — such as autobiography.

I have written about these prefaces in another place, with a view to situating
them in de Man's work, but here I want to bring them to a slightly different
conclusion.[19] Norris's aim is to defend de Man against an error "persistently"
recurring in the reception of his work. The error is exemplified by the attacks
made in the early 1980s (by Lentricchia and Eagleton) against de Man's anti-
historical, anti-meliorist, anti-political-activist bias.[20] But, according to Norris, de
Man's project has a practical component: it identifies and resists a mystifying and
at least potentially violent set of beliefs called "the aesthetic ideology." Most
plainly in his later work, says Norris, de Man practices deconstruction as a type
of engaged ideological criticism, opposed to "any kind of aesthetic idealization
that would seek to transcend history and politics in the name of some mystified
organic creed."[21]

Norris profiles this new political dimension as a result of de Man's "turn" in
mid-career — the figure of the "turn" which organizes de Man's own intellectual
biography. In his second foreword to *Blindness and Insight* (1983), de Man points
to his 1969 essay "The Rhetoric of Temporality" as constituting such a turn.[22]
"With the deliberate emphasis on rhetorical terminology, it augurs what seemed
to me to be a change, not only in terminology and in tone but in substance. This
terminology is still uncomfortably intertwined with the thematic vocabulary of
consciousness and of temporality that was current at the time, but it signals a turn
that [...] has proven to be productive."[23]

---

[18] Christopher Norris, *Paul de Man: Deconstruction and the Critique of Aesthetic Ideology*,
(New York: Routledge, 1988).

[19] "Potential Violence in Paul de Man," review article on Christopher Norris, *Paul de Man:
Deconstruction and the Critique of Aesthetic Ideology*; in: *Critical Review* 3 (1989), p. 117–137.

[20] For example, Frank Lentricchia, *Criticism and Social Change*, (Chicago: University of
Chicago Press, 1983), p. 38–52; and Terry Eagleton, *The Function of Criticism*, (London: New Left
Books, 1984), p. 149–165.

[21] Christopher Norris, *Paul de Man*, op. cit., p. 154.

[22] Paul de Man, *Blindness and Insight*, op. cit., p. 187–228.

[23] Ibidem.

The turn thereafter orientates de Man's concerns to language, with an anti-subjective, anti-humanist, anti-pathetic bias. The individual human subject figures as an opaque though ineluctable effect of language use and, hence — says de Man — is marked by an "inevitable lack of integrity."[24] It could not constitute the full authority for, and the circuit of concern of, a reading of literature, whose task is to advance into regions lying beyond "moral good conscience."[25] And there the possibility is said to arise of a suitable alternative to humanist political discourse and praxis.

When, however, Norris focuses on de Man's preface to *The Rhetoric of Romanticism* (1983), he finds a text that jeopardizes his thesis of a mid-career turn. Here de Man registers the only melancholy spectacle of chapters written over a thirty-year period that exhibit no decisive pattern, least of all a pivotal turning. Now, however, in a surprising move, Norris attempts to recoup this point for his thesis, arguing that de Man's disclaimer actually proves the turning — dialectically. If de Man here denies the existence of a turn, that is only, says Norris, because he did not want to make it too obvious to his readers. At a time before the exposure of his fascist journalism, de Man would not have wanted to call attention to an earlier period of existential self-absorption (recall "the thematic vocabulary of consciousness and of temporality"), arising from a mood of political disillusionment. He would not have wanted to suggest that he had ever had so much as to abandon "an attitude of political quietism — one that reads poetry expressly *against* all forms of delusive activist involvement."[26] Knowledge of his "turn" could inspire the question: from what fatal commitment would it have ever been necessary for him to shrink back?

At the end of his book, however, Norris actually performs a complete about-face without calling attention to it and withdraws altogether from his thesis of a turning in 1969. By postulating additional continuities in de Man's work, Norris can find traces of an attack on "organicistic" thinking even in de Man's early writings from the 1950s. This is important to do, lest the critique of aesthetic ideology, which is supposed to prove de Man's political rehabilitation, be seen as arriving too late. For without these continuities, and in the light of the disclosure of de Man's fascist journalism in 1941-42, we would, after all, be looking at a period of moral and political quiescence lasting twenty-seven years. So, at the close, Norris has to stress the combative, anti-totalizing strain in de Man's earliest critiques of the coercive implications of such poetic figures as metaphor and symbol. After political trauma and a brief quiescence, de Man, reversing direction

---

[24] Paul de Man, *Rhetoric of Romanticism*, op. cit., p. 279.

[25] Barbara Johnson attributes this phrase to de Man in *A World of Difference*, (Baltimore: Johns Hopkins University Press, 1987), p. XVII.

[26] Christopher Norris, *Paul de Man*, op. cit., p. 17.

but not mode, would presumably have gone over from one sort of activism (collaboration) to another — to the activism of the critique of aesthetic ideology. This fluctuation in Norris's argument — his preponing de Man's turn from 1969 to 1953 — is the result of his need to exonerate de Man from having too long delayed a fresh commitment to activist political criticism.[27]

As a result of these manœuvres, we are left to wonder whether de Man's allusion in *Blindness and Insight* to a productive change is a bid to gain him the authority of one who turned for the sake of truth to more rigorous, indeed "inhuman," depths; or whether de Man's late denial of a decisive turn in *The Rhetoric of Romanticism* is a bid to prove himself anti-authoritarian almost from the beginning. In *Blindness and Insight* de Man alleged that he had experienced a sort of conversion to rhetorical analysis (with all the critical and political importance that has been assigned to it). Why, then, was he unable to perceive any pattern in *The Rhetoric of Romanticism* arising from the operations of this event? Perhaps the conflict constituted a genuine aporia, perhaps he needed to have it both ways — or perhaps there is something else at stake.

What Norris fails to see throughout all his adjustments is that de Man, in the middle of his autobiographical revelations, is invoking the authority of Heidegger; the figure of the "turn" comes from Heidegger.

Of course, it was Heidegger who wrote in the "Letter on Humanism" of the "turning" which begets "[an]other [mode of] thinking." According to this mode of thinking, "every kind of anthropology and all subjectivity of man as subject is [...] left behind.[28] The turning leads thought away from the "oblivion of Being into the truth of Being," which is "the simultaneity of disclosure and concealment."[29] In positing a turn, therefore, and then in rejecting a turn, de Man is not speaking with the authority of lived experience; but neither does the authority adduced come from a believable thesis about the truthfulness of Heidegger's turn. De Man is making use of Heidegger as one who furnished a career model both good and bad — a model at once philosophically compelling but also one whose anti-humanism is bound up with his disappointed involvement in the Nazi party and fascist ideology. De Man, at the end of his life and closer to the reality of his impending exposure, would have thought twice about modelling his career on Heidegger's turn.

This is a reminder to de Man's friendly readers that they too are required to hold in the same suspicion the suspicion in which de Man himself held such

[27] Only such a commitment could constitute, for Norris, an adequate and explicit repudiation of de Man's fascist engagement in 1941–42.

[28] "On the Essence of Truth," both quotations from *Martin Heidegger: Basic Writings*, ed. David Farrell Krell, (New York: Harper & Row, 1977), p. 207 and p. 141.

[29] Martin Heidegger, *Die Technik und die Kehre*, (Pfullingen: Neske, 1962), p. 62. Second quotation from "On the Essence of Truth," in *Martin Heidegger: Basic Writings*, op. cit., p. 137.

"hybrid" autobiographical texts. These incline irresistibly to self-exculpation —
even when they are written by Paul de Man and even at the price of doing textual
violence. Such gestures produce turbulence, not models of ascetic restraint; and
such turbulence will invariably serve to mask particular intentions.[30]

In *On Grammatology*, Derrida wrote: "If it is true that writing cannot be
thought of outside the horizon of intersubjective violence, is there anything, even
science, that radically escapes it?"[31] Autobiography, certainly, as a type of reflection more turbulent than science, does not. Indeed, the place to look for the self-
articulation of de Man's autobiography is inside "the horizon of intersubjective
violence."

Here, even as we think about de Man on autobiography, we will be drawn to
the violence existing not so much between de Man's critical text and his confessional subtext as between de Man's critical text and the texts of the other
authors whom de Man reads. De Man's erratic citations, mistranslations, and mis-
prizings out of context can be read autobiographically (of course) and also must
be read this way — for only then does the impulse which informs them come to
light most clearly.[32]

De Man reads violently out of the compulsion to resist the daily, the vulgar
force of so-called empirically reliable readings. This vigilance justifies another
kind of violence — confessional anarchy being the literary-critical equivalent of
a kind of terror. Here I am guided by the logic with which Baader and Meinhof
argued for terror: terror is the visible expression of the daily violence everywhere
done but concealed, repressed, in the name of one or another unity of personhood

[30] It is more than de Man's explicit autobiographical statements that come under this head:
so do his explicit programmatic statements. Minae Mizumura puts the gist of de Man's turn as the
rigorous working out of "what is implied in his own declaration that 'the cognitive function resides
in the language and not in the subject.'" "Renunciation," *Yale French Studies* (69), p. 93. Yet a
few years later de Man declared: "I have a tendency to put upon texts an inherent authority [...].
I assume, as a working hypothesis (as a working hypothesis, because I know better than that), that
the text *knows* in an absolute way what it's doing. I know this is not the case, but it is a necessary
working hypothesis that Rousseau knows at any time what he is doing [it is supposed to be the text
that knows] and as such there is no need to deconstruct Rousseau [it is supposed to be the text that
does not need to be deconstructed]." Paul de Man, *The Resistance of Theory*, (Minneapolis:
University of Minnesota Press, 1986), p. 118. At the end of his life it was time to seem more
reasonable.

[31] Jacques Derrida, *Of Grammatology*, trans. Gayatri Spivak, (Baltimore: Johns Hopkins
University Press, 1976), p. 68.

[32] See Stanley Corngold, "Error in Paul de Man," *The Yale Critics: Deconstruction in
America*, ed. Jonathan Arac, Wlad Godzich, and Wallace Martin, (Minneapolis: University of
Minnesota Press, 1983), p. 104–106; and Theodore Ziolkowski, "The Uses and Abuses of
Romanticism," *Sewanee Review* 95 (1987), p. 276–281.

or statehood or the free market.[33] Always to read against ordinary autobiography, which treats literary works as the intentional products of empirical subjects, would be to sanction violence for a higher purpose. Terrible readings safeguard against autobiographical readings. It could seem that terrible readings are the least compromised by the suspicion that they read literature as the confession of authors. The terrible reading would prevent a reading from ever finding its way back to the security of the so-called authorial personality.[34] But in fact, as I have been reasoning, the terrible reading does not itself escape the suspicion that it is confessionally motivated.

What is at stake, in stressing the legitimacy of reading confessionally, is that a certain contract between non-violent agents (writers and readers, teachers and students) be preserved, a goal which de Man himself affirmed when he saw the entire educational process as precisely this — a contract.[35] But contracts are only as good as the force which binds them; and so the figure of the police, which is "the referent," and that referent — the police — which is a reality, sooner or later, like it or not, are bound to appear. Here it will not do any harm to reacquaint ourselves with the intellectual biography of Dostoevskij before returning to the thesis of Paul de Man's confessional anarchy — a thesis about the unreliability of autobiography, anarchically and autobiographically produced by a guilty trafficking with violence, having its own reliability as the thwarted impulse to confess.

---

[33] See Stanley Corngold, *The Fate of the Self*, (New York: Columbia University Press, 1986), p. 181–183.

[34] In "Lurid Figures" (*Reading de Man Reading*, op. cit., p. 82–104) Neil Hertz stresses de Man's distinction between violence in texts and violence in political institutions, warning that they must not be confused. But, of course, they cannot but be confused. De Man has employed every rhetorical device to confuse them throughout his writings, viz. the links between tropology and dismemberment (*The Rhetoric of Romanticism*, op. cit., p. 290), texts and revolutions (*Blindness and Insight*, op. cit., p. 165), totalization and totalitarianism (*The Resistance of Theory*, op. cit., p. 19).

[35] "I ended up finding the function of teaching in the United States — the function of an academic as distinct from the academic function — much more satisfactory than in Europe, precisely because of the contract one has with the people one teaches. Here you can actually carry out your contractual relation to them, whereas in Europe you can't." Paul de Man, *The Resistance of Theory*, op. cit., p. 115–116.

Yuan Yuan

History as Text:
Translation and Class-Consciousness in China

I N THE AUTUMN OF 1982, I was still a graduate student at a university in China, working toward my master's degree in modern American literature. Together with a handful of others, I occupied a privileged position in the censorship committee of the English Department, in charge of previewing movies imported from the "West" (Great Britain mainly). I remember one scene in a movie that later became the scandal of the University. In that scene, a "lady" and a "gentleman" were embracing in bed, both wearing discreet white loose robes. Nothing is exposed; everything is closed/clothed. Our committee closed the case with a unanimous vote: the movie passed censorship.

A week later, the movie was open to the public, to all the students of the University. This time, however, when the film reached the point of the bedroom scene, the director of the language lab deliberately blurred the focus, explaining that "This scene is not very healthy." Unfortunately, what the students saw, or believed they saw, were "two white something's doing something in bed." This unfocused obscurity set the students' imagination into full play. After the film, each student tried his or her best to reconstruct the scene from what they claimed to have seen at the vanishing point of disruption. Each student attempted to penetrate the empty space of whiteness with the projection of personal desire. Just as the students said, what is beyond the seen of the culture is not beyond imagination. Eventually, the scene was made ob-scene.

But this is not the end of the story. A few days later, thousands of versions of the film reached the ear of the school authorities. As expected, the director of the language lab was removed from his office, accused of "spreading unhealthy spiritual pollution to the younger generation in broad daylight."

BETWEEN TRANSLATION AND DISPLACEMENT:
TOWARDS A DEFINITION OF THE CHINESE PROLETARIAT

On an international scale, translation of Marxism can be categorized on two different bases: theory and practice as two forms of translation, and East and West as two locales of translation. Western Marxism, revived not long ago with the posthumous discovery of the young Marx's document, *Economic and Philosophic Manuscripts of 1844*, basically represents translation as a discourse of exile, engaged in a theoretical speculation without any social practice, although not lacking social engagement. Eastern Marxism, limited to the Soviet Union and Communist China in this context, also has suffered the effects of exile in its transgressive practice as a form of translation. Both the Soviet Union and China deviate from orthodox Marxist theory by recentering the revolutionary locale in a substitute territory: the East. The movement of this translation from theory into practice constitutes a form of displacement. Both Russia and China occupy only a marginal space within the Marxist theory of revolution. Early in this century, Russia was located in the weakest link of the capitalist chain according to Lenin's idea, as an unqualified member of the European Continent; while China, in the Far East, was not a capitalist state at all, but a semi-feudal and semi-colonial country, far from the revolutionary center of Europe. Hence, the revolutions of both Russia and China depended to a great extent upon their respective translations of Marxism, which involve theoretical translocation, practical transgression, and historical displacement. Translation, if thus considered, can be regarded as a postmodern activity, a discourse of exile and decentering, a narrative of metonymy and allegory.

In his introduction to a collection of essays entitled *Displacement*, Mark Krupnick strongly insists on the Derridian notion of translation: "There is no translation without difference."[1] Translation, in this context, seems to be an ambiguous process of negotiation between difference and indifference. From this position, translation becomes a project of objectifying difference instead of similarity, as it is often claimed. This view of translation opposes the traditional idea that translation is an enterprise attempting to bridge the gap of languages, cultures and histories, because the very transferring process is constantly subverted by the maintenance of the difference that it tries to overcome. What is inevitable in this process of recomposition is the phenomenon of sequential substitutions: a metonymic discourse. Consequently, the metonymic displacement becomes the keynote of translation.

In the 1920's, when the Chinese Communist movement took shape, there were but a handful of industrial workers in China, not at all enough to constitute an independent class, still less a class consciousness. If "workers" in the Marxist text had been rendered as "workers" in its Chinese version, this signifier would not have drawn sufficient people to promote the Chinese revolution. Thus, the translation from "workers" into "proletarians" should not be simply dismissed as a mistake of the translator, but viewed as a vital strategy that made possible the Chinese Communist revolution. It is a way to, if not a way of, Marxism.

---

[1] Mark Krupnick, *Displacement: Derrida and After*, (Bloomington: Indiana UP, 1983), Introduction, p. 6.

As commonly defined, proletarians can refer to both the lowest social and economic class of a community, and to the class of the industrial workers who lack their own means of production and sell their labour to live: the wage-labourers. In the context of European history, "proletarians" definitely refers to the latter — the workers who are, simultaneously, of the lowest social and economic class. There is no inherent contradiction between these two classes of people in this definition. However, in the context of Chinese history, "proletarians" only implies the former, which contains the latter. In the early part of the 20th century, the majority of the lowest class of the Chinese community was constituted by the peasants, who fared much worse than the workers. Defined within the framework of European history, "proletarians" would exclude the peasants; while in Chinese history, the definition would abandon the workers to a marginal corner and replace the peasants at the very center. Thus the equivalent relationship between the two classes of people in European history and the inclusive relationship between them in Chinese history constitutes the metonymic displacement of translation.

Through this linguistic and historical substitution, the outmoded class in the orthodox Marxist notion of history, constituted by the peasants, is translated into a revolutionary class functioning as the leading power in shaping Chinese Marxist history. This makeup of the Chinese proletarians and their makeup of Chinese Communist history reveal a subtle but vital distortion of the Marxist theory of the proletariat. Essentially, the peasants, rather than the workers, are revolutionized to advance a Communist cause in China. Hence, when "workers" is changed into "proletarians" in the Chinese version of *The Communist Manifesto*, this supposedly unquestionable and unequivocal word, with a shift of historical and geographical referents, becomes in translation a word at play, of indeterminacy, ambiguity, and difference between East and West.

It is evident that translation, in this case, has to do away with the notion of lack, by turning absence into presence. As J.-B. Pontalis remarks: "The translator is always an agent of *in other words*."[2] This means the metonymic slippage between the original word and the translated is an inevitable movement of re-writing regulated by the subjectivity of the translator. Pontalis psychoanalyzes the process by focusing on the issue of the "cathected area" in translation: "Stumbling against the precise obstacle in translation, the gap between the two languages reveals the presence of a sensitive point and a specifically cathected area deriving its meaning from the author's personal life."[3] Accordingly, "workers," as defined in the Marxist text, is the most sensitive point in the Chinese Communist

---

[2] J.B. Pontalis, *Frontiers in Psychoanalysis: Between the Dream and Psychic Pain* (New York: International UP, 1981) p. 148.

[3] Ibidem, p. 149.

revolution; the Chinese revolutionary agent has to play with the signifier "proletarians" as a substitute for the original "workers" in order to avoid "stumbling against the precise obstacle" — lack of workers in the Chinese revolution. The interchangeability of workers and proletarians in European history and the uninterchangeability of them in Chinese history expose the secret of the Chinese translation of Marxism and its displacement. The borderline between presence and absence, inclusion and exclusion, similarity and difference is obscured in the intermediate area between translation and displacement. So the Chinese proletariat is from the very beginning a supplement, a substitute for the ideal subject of Marxist history — the workers.

Translation is a narrative composed in the tropes of metonymy and allegory. The traditional notion of translation valorizes and iconizes the romantic value of intersubjectivity, correspondence, and sympathy; while the postmodern idea of translation deconstructs this myth of coincidence by emphasizing distance and difference.

In *Blindness and Insight*, Paul de Man offers us a model for distinguishing the allegorical mode of discourse from the symbolic one. The allegorical differs from the romantic in that the former stresses distance and difference, whereas the latter insists on coincidence and identification. The romantic view of translation is based on a symbolic relationship between the original and the translated, relying upon the transcending power of the signifier, the myth of organic unity, and the possibility of coincidence. De Man explains:

> In the world of the symbol it would be possible for the image to coincide with the substance, since the substance and its representation do not differ in their being [...]. Their relationship is one of simultaneity, which, in truth, is spatial in kind, and in which the intervention of time is merely a matter of contingency, whereas, in the world of allegory, time is the originary constitutive category [...]. It remains necessary, if there is to be allegory, that the allegorical sign refer to another sign that precedes it. The meaning constituted by the allegorical sign can then consist only in the *repetition* (in the Kierkegaardian sense of the term) of a previous sign with which it can never coincide, since it is of essence of this previous sign to be pure anteriority.[4]

The Chinese translation of Marxism demonstrates exactly this allegorical mode of discourse because the coincidence between the histories of East and West is impossible. Hence, the difference of temporality is of ultimate importance. "Workers" can never coincide with "peasants," even if they are placed under the same signifier "proletarians." They indicate totally different classes of people in different historical and social contexts. Actually, the translator of Marxism in

---

[4] Paul de Man, *Blindness and Insight: Essays in the Rhetoric of Contemporary Criticism* (Minneapolis: U of Minnesota P, 1986) p. 207.

China is attempting no less than to deny the disparity of history between East and West, and to bridge the gap between feudalism and capitalism.

Consequently, translation becomes an endeavour to trans-late. There is no possibility of coincidence, correspondence, and identification, but a display of discontinuity, disruption, and decontexuality. As de Man puts it: "Whereas the symbol postulates the possibility of an identity or identification, allegory designates primarily a distance in relation to its own origin, and, renouncing the nostalgia and the desire to coincide, it establishes its language in the void of this temporal difference."[5] Because of the historical distance between them, the "proletarians" of China can hardly identify themselves with the European workers. The translation of Marxism is made possible only in this "void of the temporal difference," as if East and West share a simultaneous and organic history without any significant difference. Translation of Marxism in China thus becomes a translation of difference in indifference.

In this allegorical mode, translation has to obviate the original in order to start a new life. In "The Task of the Translator," Walter Benjamin says, "a translation issues from the original — not so much from its life as from its afterlife."[6] That is, the original has to die in order to live in a new context, as a form of postponement and deferral. The translator has to dispose of the dead body of the original and relocate a new body to incarnate the spirit. "For in its afterlife — which could not be called that if it were not a transformation and a renewal of something living — the original undergoes a change," Benjamin writes. "Even a word with fixed meaning can undergo a maturing process."[7] Thus, "proletarians" in the Western context, with a fixed meaning (workers), metamorphoses into "peasants" as signified in the Eastern context, but with an ironic overtone, because it is not so much a "maturing process" as it is an anti-historical regression, from workers who are elevated as the representatives of the advanced productive power to peasants who are degraded as the outmoded class dropping out of history in Marxist historical materialism.

According to Benjamin, translation, unlike the work of literature, is never at the center of the "language forest." Instead, translation "calls into it [the language forest] without entering, aiming at that single spot where echo is able to give, in its own language, the reverberation of the work in the alien one."[8] Here Benjamin's phrase "the single spot" sounds like Pontalis' notion of the "cathected area." "Proletarians" is exactly the echo that is produced in translation. Only

---

[5] Ibidem, p. 207.

[6] Walter Benjamin, "The Task of the Translator," *Illuminations* (New York: Schockem Books, 1969) p. 71.

[7] Ibidem, p. 73.

[8] Ibidem, p. 76.

"proletarians" (the echo), rather than "workers" (the original), can possibly produce in China the reverberation that stirs the majority of people into political action. So the Chinese revolution, modelled on this translation, is turned into a distant echo of Marxism, with historical deformation and social transfiguration.

As we see, the translation of Marxism in China is a discourse of metonymy and allegory, with a special ironic symptom of regression. It is anachronistically as well as anti-chronistically achieved, if a diachronic relationship has to be maintained instead of a synchronic one. Displacement is at the center of Marxist discourse and its practice in China.

In the linguistic realm, translation is a recomposition of signifiers, concerning the questions of codification, contextuality, and referentiality. In an economic sense, translation is also a process of importation, involved with consumption and reproduction. It is a phenomenon of cultural exchange if not intercourse.

The translation of Marxism can be considered as an activity of consumption and reproduction of meaning in China. The translatability of Marxism does not depend so much upon historical objectivity as upon the desire of the translating subject, the consumer who only wants to import its applicability and availability. The value of the imported product lies in its exchange, not its life but its afterlife: the value for sale. The consumer always tries to find his own image reflected in the imported product in order to claim it as his own, or he asserts his ego by re-authorization during the process of importation. The translator is never absent in this importation process because the original product is filtered and refracted through the center of the regulating subject. The original often becomes evacuated or decentered while undergoing the transformation of decontexualization and re-contexualization. With personal selection and desire, the translator can scarcely escape self-reflexivity and dissemination in conducting this transitional recomposition. After all, Marxism is a product of the West, and for the West. The Chinese translator has to Easternize and naturalize it (or historicize it possibly) to render it applicable and attractive to the Chinese market.

If Marxism can be regarded as a commodity of signs, then this commodity becomes a totally detached free object for exchange, divorced from its historical referent and transgressing its original signification. Whoever consumes it can find meaning in it to be appropriated that is completely dissociated from the original reality. Translation exhibits exactly this phenomenon because it detaches the signifier from its original context, and re-authorizes it for sale in the new market. Any kind of translation is an "interested" translation, with the purpose of producing surplus value. Clearly, "proletarians" is the interested word of investment which yields the highest surplus value in the production of the Chinese Communist revolution.

The process of translation happens in the third space — the imaginary space mediated by the play of signifiers, characterized as a dialectics of presence and absence, a negotiation of evacuation and supplementarity. What Jean Baudrillard critiques of the political economy in *The Mirror of Production* can be applied to translation as well: "The signifieds and the referents are now abolished to the sole profit of the play of signifiers, of a generalized formalization in which the code no longer refers back to any subjective or objective 'reality,' but to its own logic."[9] Accordingly, in the Chinese translation of Marxism, the historical referent (European history) is brushed away, and the subjective reality (workers) and the objective reality (capitalist society) are removed from the scene. With a shift of referent, the original is pushed to the obscure horizon, and the word "proletarians," decontextualized in the new environment, obtains a new meaning in the recontextualized code of signification — the feudal code of China. In this active manipulation of signs in the chain of the signifiers, the material substantiality of the sign is entirely dissolved in the bi-textual play of translation. Devoid of its substance, the sign is at the disposal of the code of signification. Consequently, what is translated into Chinese is not the material object, but an allegorical meaning produced in the frame of a feudal code. So the signifier "proletarians," detached from its signified "workers" with a shift of referent, is re-codified in a new system of signification dominated by the feudal ethos. As a result, the European proletarians are translated as the equivalent of the Chinese peasants: an irony of translation and importation.

Translation is a project of transplantation, displacement and domestication. It does not depend so much upon inter-subjectivity as upon the lack of it. Translation often is turned into an objectification of the difference, distance and dissociation which it desires to overcome, therefore exhibiting a paradoxical movement of irony, metonymy and allegory. Translation creates difference instead of dissolving it and maintains the distance instead of surmounting it.

When "workers" is translated into "proletarians" in the Chinese (per)version of *The Communist Manifesto*, it is not a mistake of the translator, but a critical strategy of the Chinese revolution. Supposedly, if Marxism committed an ethnocentric sin by excluding the East as the center of revolution, then China is obliged to restore "true Marxism" by translating its meaning within the context of Chinese history. If "Workers of the world, unite" is the voice originating from the ethnocentric center of Europe, China has to produce an echo against this center; otherwise China has nothing to offer to replenish this theoretical space of Marxism. Thus, the Chinese revolution is transformed into an apology for history and an echo of reality.

Actually, Marxism was introduced to China under the despotic signifier of science. It has been extolled as the truth of history, as the universal signifier of the Absolute (between science and myth). It was first transported to China as scientific fact proved by the Russian revolution. Therefore, Marxism entered China

---

[9] Jean Baudrillard, *The Mirror of Production* (St. Louis: Telos P, 1975) p. 127.

via the translation of the Russian revolution, and then the Chinese revolution
became a translation of a translation, a double displacement.

PRODUCTION OF CLASSES AND CLASS CONSCIOUSNESS:
SELF AND OTHER IN QUESTION

When the unprecedented proletarian cultural revolution started in 1966, Mao
proclaimed that the goal of the fatal revolution was to eradicate the bourgeois
class as well as bourgeois class consciousness from Chinese native soil. It was a
massive political movement proposed as the necessary step to erase bourgeois
class consciousness and enhance proletarian class consciousness. But it is common
knowledge that China only temporarily and indirectly experienced the historical
stage of capitalism in its territory. One feels obliged to inquire why bourgeois
class consciousness was so powerfully influential that the Communist Party of
China was forced to wage a ten-year "cultural revolution" to uproot it.

   Class and class consciousness are the two fundamental concepts that Marx
created in his theory of historical materialism to analyze the development of
capitalism in particular and the development of human society in general. However, the application of this theory to the analysis of pre-capitalist societies has
met with strong resistance and discontent. A complicated semi-feudal and semi-
colonial society such as China, if forced to employ these two concepts to image
itself, would have to rewrite its own version of class and class consciousness
within the frame of its own social conditions and economic structure. This re-
formed text of Chinese history, in terms of Marxist historical materialism, would
mean that the objective historical structure of feudal and colonial society would
have to be reframed by the subjective doctrine of capitalist society. Consequently,
social classifications of the Chinese community are reduced by the Chinese
communists to fit in the two dominant signifiers — proletariat and bourgeoisie —
as the dialectical powers of history-making.

   When the Communist movement started up in China in the early 1920's, China
was still a semi-feudal and semi-colonial society in which the majority of the
population were peasants. If there were but a small number of workers, the
bourgeoisie were certainly fewer. To classify them as the two major contradictory
powers of Chinese society is simply to overlook the main issue of Chinese history
and its native situation. Nevertheless, Chinese Marxists had to construct the
proletarian class and the bourgeois class in this way if the Chinese revolution were
to be qualified as a Marxist movement.

   The re-classification of all the "exploited and repressed" in Chinese society has
been achieved under the unifying signifier "proletariat," which in Chinese simply
means the "have-not"-class, a loose term indicating workers, peasants and
lumpens. The bourgeois class means the "have"-class, including capitalists,

landlords, businessmen and intellectuals to a certain extent. There is no denying that the dominant part of the proletariat consists of peasants.

The classical view of peasants as a social class is still a critical issue in contemporary debate among Chinese Marxist theoreticians. In *The Eighteenth Brumaire of Louis Bonaparte*, Marx himself assumes a very ambivalent stance toward peasants as a class: "In so far as millions of families live under economic conditions of existence that separate their mode of life, their interests and their culture from those of other classes, and put them in hostile opposition to the latter, they form a class. In so far as there is merely a local interconnection among the small-holding peasants and the identity of their interests begets no community, no national bond and no political organization, they do not form a class."[10] This is as much as saying that even though economically the peasants constitute a class, politically they do not. In other words, as a class they do not fit properly into Marxist theory.

In *The Mirror of Production*, Baudrillard observes: "The concept of class is a universalist and rationalist concept, born in a society of rational production and of the calculation of productive forces [...]. To make a class of the proletariat is hence to enclose it in an order of definition (characterized by 'class consciousness' as 'the subject of history')."[11] Since China has not yet reached the stage of capitalist rational production, the class concept is without question an imported ideological product instead of an inherent emergence from its own history.

In *History and Class Consciousness*, Georg Lukacs also comments on this issue: "Thus class consciousness has quite a different relation to history in pre-capitalist and capitalist periods. In the former case the classes could only be deduced from the immediately given historical reality *by the method of historical materialism.* In capitalism they themselves constitute this immediately given historical *reality.*"[12] This passage suggests that the production of classes in a feudal society is but a rational deduction mediated through the mirror of "historical materialism," or a historical recollection from the position of capitalist reference — a rational mode of production indeed. Marxism came to China under the despotic signifier of science and universal truth, but "through its most 'scientific' inclinations toward earlier societies, it [historical materialism] naturalizes them under the sign of the mode of production."[13] Apparently another case of scientific myth that needs deconstruction.

---

[10] Karl Marx, *The Eighteenth Brumaire of Louis Bonaparte* (New York: International Publishers, 1977) p. 124.

[11] Jean Baudrillard, *The Mirror of Production*, op. cit., p. 156-157.

[12] Georg Lukacs, *History and Class Consciousness: Studies in Marxist Dialectics* (Massachusetts: MIT P, 1968) p. 58.

[13] Jean Baudrillard, *The Mirror of Production*, op. cit., p. 90.

In capitalist society, class is an immediately experienced phenomenon, whereas in pre-capitalist societies, class is merely an analytical concept, a rational construct, an ideological import detached from its historical objectivity, and an abstract notion produced in the manipulation of signs. It is under the power of this sign framed within this theoretical model that China has had to collect and re-collect its social classes. The proletarian class in China is not a historical product, but an ideological invention imported and imposed on Chinese history from outside. As Baudrillard says: "It is no longer a question of 'being' oneself but of producing oneself, from conscious activity to the primitive productions of desire."[14]

If the proletarian class is reproduced from historical re-collection by the method of historical (im)materialism, then the bourgeois class is also an invention, mainly reconstructed from two historical recollections.

First of all, the bourgeois class, as a concept, is an ethical construction from the historical residue of the feudal culture of China. Historically, the conception of this class has been associated with the traditional image of Chinese traders who are not scholars, not laborers, and not soldiers, but middle-men or meddle-men. In the light of traditional Chinese ethics, Confucianism in the main, traders are cast in the most despised positions in society since they are after money rather than knowledge, engaged in exchange instead of production, promoting circulation instead of stability. Essentially, they constitute a dangerous free element in a tightly structured hierarchical society. Because they are the most mobile and most unstructured members of society, they exercise an unpredictable, uncontrollable impact upon the stable feudal community of self-sufficiency. Thus the concept of the bourgeois class has been established on the basis of a feudal code which defines a group of people as the "other" through the reflection of Chinese conventions.

Secondly, the bourgeois class, both as concept and in existence, is a phenomenon of foreign importation. Historically, it can be traced back to the period of Western colonization of feudal China. Foreign businessmen, after their guns forced open the gate of the forbidden empire of the East, rushed to this vast territory, seduced by its cheap labour and rich sources, and later fattened by ruthless exploitation and cruel extraction. This barbarian, devilish image of Western businessmen as colonialists obviously is more powerful — more real and more alive — to the Chinese people than the concept defined in Marxist textbooks along class lines. So the materialization of the concept "bourgeois" has been associated historically with an image of the West presenting itself as the other of the Chinese empire.

---

[14] Ibidem, p. 19.

Hence, the conception of the bourgeois class is connected synchronically with the other of the East (Western colonialists), and diachronically with the other of feudal China (the nonproductive traders). The other positions itself as the Terror to the holy family of China — the central kingdom. To paraphrase Edward Said's notion of orientalism, capitalism in China "existed as a set of values attached, not to its modern realities, but to a series of valorized contacts it had had with a distant European past."[15] Finally, the Marxist concept of bourgeois class, when imported into China, dissolves its material reality and becomes a vacant signifier detached from its historical referentiality to the West; it is re-substantiated with the historical residues of the East and its historical image of the West.

If the classes in China are recollected and re-assembled within the structuralist frame of Marxist historical materialism, and characterized as a process of re-organization of Chinese society through the ethnocentric mirror of European history, then the class consciousness of both proletarian and bourgeois is but a postponed theoretical concept, an ideological construct, and a historical deferral.

One is obliged to question the possibility and validity of the emergence of class consciousness in an agrarian and feudal society of China if class consciousness is generally considered a historical phenomenon of the modern age, connected with the new technology of the Industrial Revolution, labor division, free market, commodification of labor and socialization of production. Most Marxists agree that "class consciousness is a phenomenon of the modern industrial era."[16] But at the time of the Communist revolution, China was still a feudal society in which the peasants as an economic class were isolated, land-bound and self-sufficient. They did not constitute the modern age, nor represent the advanced productive force. In the previous section, we observed that Marx simply dismissed peasants as a class on a political basis. Thus, class consciousness is merely a lack in Chinese society and Chinese history. How could class consciousness emerge without the existence of class itself and the necessary social conditions as its prerequisites?

"The outlook of the other classes (petty bourgeois or peasants)," Lukacs argues, "is ambiguous or sterile because their existence is not based exclusively on their role in the capitalist system of production but is indissolubly linked with the vestiges of feudal society. Their aim, therefore, is not to advance capitalism or to transcend it, but to reverse its action or at least to prevent it from developing fully."[17] Lukacs has a point here, but rather ironically. The Chinese proletariat constituted by peasants did "reverse its action" by successfully preventing

---

[15] Edward Said, *Orientalism* (New York: Vintage Books, 1979) p. 85.

[16] E.J. Hosbawm, "Class Consciousness in History," *Aspects of History and Class Consciousness*, ed. Istvan Meszaros (London: Routledge & Kegan Paul, 1971) p. 7.

[17] Georg Lukacs, *History and Class Consciousness*, op. cit., p. 59.

capitalist development in their country for half a century, but China now is attempting to redeem that reversal through present reforms: modernization and Westernization. True to Lukacs' words, the peasants functioning as the proletarian class of China are "indissolubly linked with the vestiges of feudal society," namely, the ideological foundations of proletarian class consciousness in China.

In *History and Class Consciousness*, Lukacs remarks: "Class consciousness is the 'ethics' of the proletariat, the unity of its theory and practice."[18] Ironically, the production of proletarian class consciousness in China has to reverse this order because it is the ethics of the proletariat (peasants) — a fundamental feudal ethics of the East — that determines their class consciousness. Ideologically, class consciousness thus composed within the code of the Chinese conventional value system advocates first of all the virtue of self-denial and self-negation in order to serve the Communist common cause. The feudal values of devotion, loyalty, piousness and commitment are turned into the essence of proletarian class consciousness. Actually, it is not a form of self-consciousness, but the very abolishment of it. Another paradoxical movement of construction and destruction.

The subjectivity of the proletarian thus constructed under the sign of class consciousness virtually is a non-self, a negation of subjectivity and a renunciation of consciousness. To "be" a proletarian means not to "have" anything. Locked within the code of their "have-not"-class, the proletarians are trained to disown everything, especially themselves. As a result of this ideological re-construction of the non-self, their desires, bodies and ideas are all owned by the government as a confirmation of public ownership. In the constant political movements to purify bourgeois class consciousness, the proletarians are re-educated to deny their bodies, disown their desires and possess nothing. Thus dispossessed, they are converted into nothing, and nothingness becomes their existential state of being, living in an unauthentic condition of false consciousness. The tragedy is not so much that they do not have a self, as they do not even have the sense or the memory of ever possessing one. This knowledge of self is totally abolished; the desire for it completely banned. In their minds, to "have" is to "be" bourgeois. Finally it is not a political consciousness, but a political non-consciousness that dominates their action.

However, self-denial is not an easy enterprise for anyone, including the Chinese "proletarians." This "historical subject" has been forced to raise its class consciousness continuously by way of education camps, education propaganda, and education campaigns. Here the question of class consciousness is simplified as a question of learning, a product of knowledge, a creation of ideological apparatuses, and an illusion of reality. It is thus extremely ironic when Lukacs says: "In view of the great distance that the proletariat has to travel ideologically

---

[18] Ibidem, p. 42.

it would be disastrous to foster any illusions."[19] Paradoxically, ideology, originally regarded as the power to avoid illusion, objectifies the formation of illusion and later delusion. Lukacs insists: "The fate of the revolution (and with it the fate of mankind) will depend on the ideological maturity of the proletariat, i.e. on its class consciousness."[20] Ironically enough, the class consciousness of the Chinese proletariat matures ideologically by regression to feudal ethics. Class consciousness thus raised can only help the historical subject divorce itself from historical objectivity and concrete social situations, living in an ideologically fabricated space of Utopia, a form of self-deception. It is quite true when Louis Althusser remarks: "Ideology, then, for Marx an imaginary assemblage (bricolage), is a pure dream, empty and vain, constituted by the 'day's residues'"[21] — the feudal ethos. "What is represented in ideology" Althusser argues, "is therefore not the system of the real relations which govern the existence of individuals, but the imaginary relations of those individuals to the real relations in which they live."[22] Ideological construction constitutes alienation rather than identification, displacement rather than replacement.

The production of the class consciousness of both bourgeois and proletariat is an ideological process within the structuralistic limit of historical materialism, evacuated of its historical materiality, divorced from the historical context. If proletarian class consciousness is substantiated by the feudal ethics of Chinese culture to fit into the Marxist theoretical framework, then bourgeois class consciousness is structured in an antithetical position, a product in the hands of dialecticians, not necessarily existential, but certainly logical. From its very emergence, bourgeois class consciousness has occupied the position of the other, historically and ideologically, diachronically and synchronically.

As we see, the class consciousness of both proletariat and bourgeois is structured within the subjective framework of the self that consists of Chinese proletarian ethics. Consequently, the other, the bourgeois class consciousness, turns out to be no more than a reflection of the self, or other-self that is both repressed and desired while the real other is displaced and discharged. This ideological other is but an alienating and alienated element that poses itself as a threat to the self. Therefore, the difference between them is not a real one, but a binary construct, representing the two faces of the same coin. Their respective identities are not achieved through the principle of difference at all, but through discrimination and differentiation with the self at the center as reference. Therefore the real other is

---

[19] Ibidem, p. 80.

[20] Ibidem, p. 70.

[21] Louis Althusser, "Ideology and Ideological State Apparatuses," *Critical Theory Since 1965*, ed. Hazard Adams (Tallahassee: UP of Florida, 1986) p. 240.

[22] Ibidem, p. 242.

excluded at the moment it is defined in this self-perpetuated discourse. The other is constructed for the self and of the self with the other's absence. For lack of a historical existence, bourgeois class consciousness is defined negatively against what the proletarians believe they are not — a typical revolutionary discourse of negativity. The continual negation of bourgeois class consciousness in repeated political campaigns since the founding of Communist China only positively affirms the existence of the repressed other-self. At last bourgeois class consciousness, filtered and assimilated through proletarian class consciousness, becomes domesticated, naturalized and exoticized simultaneously. This process is carried on as a form of colonization and incarnation. Consequently, the ideological image overrules the empirical being, and the subjective artifact displaces the objective fact.

As the other of the Chinese feudal history, bourgeois class consciousness embodies what is denied the self in feudal ethics — freedom, pleasure, and desire. Anti-bourgeois class struggles (including the Cultural Revolution) are actually projects to purify the body of its desire, forbid the body its pleasure and deprive the body of its freedom. Thus bourgeois class consciousness, as a linguistic term signifying anything at all, marks the border to the proletarians, the border of both seduction and condemnation, the border of an unknown self. Either way, the term "bourgeois," as class or class consciousness, suffers from not being real, and there is absolutely no promise of return to the authentic being. As de Man says: "The ironic language split the subject into an empirical self that exists in a state of inauthenticity and a self that exists only in the form of a language that asserts the knowledge of this inauthenticity."[23] Finally, bourgeois class consciousness becomes "the sign [which] no longer designates anything at all. It approaches its true structural limit which is to refer back only to other signs. All reality then becomes the place of a semi-urgical manipulation, of a structural simulation."[24]

Bourgeois class consciousness is also a political project, if not a political projection, of Occidentalism because of the distance and difference between the two cultures. This imaginary relationship between them also reveals the unbalanced power relationship between East and West. The West, in its intercourse with the East, is generally regarded as the terror associated with the image of colonialism. The bourgeois class, as the embodiment of Western values, is constructed in a systematic representation within the Chinese "regime of truth." The basic bourgeois values — freedom, individuality and commodification — simply are not congenial to the Chinese agrarian culture which stresses closure, depersonalization and the hierarchical structuring of human relationships.

[23] Paul de Man, *Blindness and Insight*, p. 214.

[24] Jean Baudrillard, *The Mirror of Production*, p. 128.

Certainly, all human societies have the same tendency to name that which can not be accepted, and that which poses threats to itself, as alien, evil and other. However, the Chinese eventually found a specific external model to represent the corruptive power of the other to the East. America was selected to materialize this image because it has long been denounced in Chinese revolutionary discourse as the locale of "free sex," the most condemned and desired object in the feudal code of China. Thus freedom is reduced to free sex: the image distorts the content as the signifier is totally split from the signified. "Bourgeois" is reconstituted, reassembled, crafted, in short, born out of proletarian efforts.[25] The silenced other is totally at the mercy of the voiced self. Finally, bourgeois class consciousness is feudalized and exoticized in its absence. Under the gaze of the self, the other is petrified and transformed into a dead body.

The political exoticism or otherism of bourgeois class consciousness is actually a project to enlarge distance and difference — to increase the hostility and the terror of the other, thereby mystifying the relationship in between. A case of cultural terrorism. The West becomes a projection from the Eastern ethnocentric center, a product of rational deduction and imaginative supplementation. The bourgeois turns out to be an alien creature created in the cultural lab, like Frankenstein. Said's critique of Orientalism can be applied to Occidentalism here as well, but in a reverse position: "It domesticated this knowledge to the West, filtering it through regulating codes, classifications, specimen cases, periodical reviews, dictionaries [...], translations, all of which together formed a simulacrum of the Orient and reproduced it materially in the West for the West."[26] Occidentalism undergoes a similar process of knowledge production with the exception that the enterprise engages much more fear and desire in the East than in the West because of the unequal power relationship between them. Hence, the production of class consciousness is a complicated project of political investment, dominated by the desires and interests of proletarians. Eventually, the bourgeois class molded through the efforts of the proletariat turns out to be no more than another instead of the other. In this process of otherism, the proletariat victimizes both itself and its opponent since the former falls into a self-laid delusion while the latter suffers distortion, displacement and disregard. A case of Orientalism/Occidentalism.

After all it is capitalism that materializes class and class consciousness in history. As Lukacs says, "the rule of the bourgeoisie means the abolition of the

---

[25] This paragraph is a parody of Said's idea of Orientalism. The original version runs like this: "The Oriental was reconstituted, reassembled, crafted, in short, born out of the orientalist efforts", (87).

[26] Edward Said, *Orientalism*, p. 166.

estates-system and this leads to the organization of society along class lines."[27] After China established socialism in 1949, it still attempted to organize its society along class lines by producing two opposing classes in an ideological form, anti-chronistically and anachronistically. The stronger the negation of the bourgeois, the stronger its existence, a negative affirmation. Apparently, Marxism as an European text, if mis-placed in the hands of the Eastern reader, can produce nothing but misreading and miss-meaning. In this production of class conscious-ness, Chinese Communists also reversed the most basic Marxist doctrine of historical materialism, which stipulates clearly that it is the economic infra-structure (agrarian in the case of China) that determines the superstructure (feudal). But political practice in China contradicts this process because it is the superstructure (the ideologically-produced false consciousness and historical subject) that determines the present form of Chinese society. Historical materialism is thus historically dematerialized.

Actually the whole enterprise of class and class consciousness is conducted in the third space, the imaginary space of ideology, spreading over the intermediate territory of cultural and historical difference between East and West. This ideological space can be characterized as a realm of both fixity and fantasy, constitutive of an imaginary relationship. As Althusser states: "Ideology is conceived as a pure illusion, a pure dream, i.e. as nothingness. All its reality is external to it. Ideology is thus thought as an imaginary construction whose status is exactly like the theoretic status of the dream among writers before Freud."[28]

As we see, the ideological makeup of class and class consciousness is a political project of transfiguring history. We then need to ask: Who is supposed to be the subject of history? In China, the proletarian, while objectifying the bourgeois as the other of the self (or other-self), also produces the subject of itself. In defining itself as the subject of history, the proletarian subjugates all other "subjects" under itself. The center of the proletarian power is thus established through this process of ideological subjectivization. Althusser remarks:

> We observe that the structure of all ideology, interpellating individuals as subjects in the name of a Unique and Absolute Subject is *specular*, i.e. a mirror-structure, and *doubly* specular: this mirror duplication is constitutive of ideology and ensures its functioning. Which means that all ideology is *centered*, that the Absolute Subject occupies the unique place of the Center, and interpellates around it the infinity of individuals into subjects in a double mirror-connexion such that it *subjects* the subjects to the Subject, while giving them in the subject in which each subject can contemplate its own image (present and future) the *guarantee* that this really concerns them and Him.[29]

---

[27] Georg Lukacs, *History and Class Consciousness*, op. cit., p. 55.

[28] Louis Althusser, *Critical Theory Since 1965*, op. cit., p. 240.

[29] Ibidem, p. 248.

At last, the image of the bourgeois class is but an-other image of the proletariat itself, a dialectic double of self-reflexivity.

Finally, the critique of class and class consciousness is finished with the deconstruction of the unquestionable metaphysical presence in Chinese history — the existence of proletariat and bourgeoisie. The production of class and class consciousness is a political project, a historical postponement, and an ideological otherism conducted and confirmed by the self-entitled Subject of history — the proletariat, while real Chinese history is constituted elsewhere.

DISPLACEMENT OF MARXISM:
CHINESE HISTORY UNDER RECONSTRUCTION

The Communist Manifesto of 1847 begins: "A spectre is haunting Europe — the spectre of Communism."[30] One century later, this spectre has possessed the body of the East and transformed it into a demon. The practice of Marxism in the Eastern territory (Russia and China) once changed the world's political and economic structure and split the world into two major camps: capitalism and communism.

Marxism, the spectre that haunts Europe, was originally a product of Western culture, by the West and for the West. To universalize it as the transcendental signifier of history is to make a religion out of history, and a myth out of "science." To extol Marxism as the holy text deciphering all the codes of history is to commit the sin of rationalism and fanaticism. Marxism, rightly viewed, is but one of the many interpretations of the development of history in terms of production. The West thus conceived in the Marxist discourse is already a translation and displacement of Western history. China, if constructed in this light of historical materialism, inevitably suffers double displacement in its translation. To reproduce the Chinese social structure and native history within the frame of Marxist ideology would be another case of Orientalism/Occidentalism (but which one?). To rearrange feudal China along class lines would push real history into an unmarked corner of oblivion. Marxism belongs to another history and another culture, another continent and another tongue. To make China a communist country in terms of Marxism is to sacrifice both China and Marxism.

In modern Chinese history, the practice of Marxism is the first powerful encounter of ideologies between East and West, a collision of their cultures as well. Historically, Marxism spread to China via the Eastern territory of Russian revolution, as a proof of scientific truth. So Marxism occupies a special position

---

[30] Karl Marx and Friedrich Engels, *The Communist Manifesto* (New York: Pathfinder P, 1970), p. 16.

between myth and truth in its intercourse with feudal China. The Chinese revolutionaries gained knowledge of Marxism more through the direct social practices of Russia than through theoretical speculation. This "spreading" makes the Chinese revolution a rather ambiguous movement: Eastward or Westward?

China, originally the illegal body in Marxist text, is turned into a maternal body for its reproduction. Like a decayed body of an old civilization, China endures the penetration of Western Utopianism and produces an illegitimate feudal Communism, after many abortive labours to reform its society. This intercourse between East and West is a case of ideological transplantation, cultural colonialism, and violent disruption of Chinese history. The Chinese historical structure is displaced, deformed and disembodied by the Chinese communists's appropriation of the power of Western ideology. The East is regarded as an extension of Western history, which creates the counter-history of East.

In this dislocated territory of Marxism, China suffers the lack of both historical subject (workers) and historical circumstances (capitalism), since both of them are phenomena signified in Western history. Eventually, Marxism produces the desire to be masters of history in the Eastern subject (peasants), but refuses any possibility of that subject's identification with the Western ideal ego (workers). This alienation, activated by the ideological importation, creates an absence of being. This process of Western importation violently disrupts the traditional ecology and historical continuity of Chinese society. But this transformation of the social structure in China is not so much the result of changing the mode of production, as Marx claims in *German Ideology*. Instead, it resides in the very power of ideology in his critique. Marx observes:

> The further the separate spheres, which act on one another, extend in the course of this development and the more the original isolation of the separate nation-alities is destroyed by the advanced mode of production, by intercourse and by the natural division of labour between various nations arising as a result, the more history becomes world history. Thus, for instance, if in England a machine is invented which deprives countless workers of bread in India and China, and over-turns the whole form of existence of those empires, this invention becomes a world-historical fact [...]. From this it follows that this transformation of history into world history is by no means a mere abstract act on the part of 'self-con-sciousness,' the world spirit, or of any other metaphysical spectre, but a quite material, empirically veritable fact [...].[31]

When the Chinese social form is restructured according to Marxist historical materialism, Chinese history is translated, by the same principle, into a world history — a thoroughly Westernized history. Thus dislocated, China is on its way to losing its historical continuity, natural ecology and cultural identity. Eastern

---

[31] Karl Marx, "German Ideology," *Karl Marx/Friedrich Engels: Collected Works*, Vol. 5 (New York: International Publishers, 1976), p. 50-51.

history is lost in the receding horizon of this Westward movement, and there is no return or eternal return. In this unequal exchange of cultures, the East is sacrificed to the West because the West assumes the position of authority and truth; whereas the East is reduced to the position of a text, misread and mis-written. In this translation, Eastern identity is discarded and deformed to re-identify itself with the Western ego, which functions as the universal self of the world. At long last, Chinese history will be lost in its Westward movement. No East, but West.

Even from an epistemological view of methods, the East cannot escape the West. Clearly, China has constantly been trying to control the Marxist text by domestication, naturalization and simulation. However, the whole process of translation is controlled by the so-called scientific methods of Western knowledge. The very terminology that offers China an identity in its Marxist text is produced in the West according to Western history and society. To define China in terms of Western concepts constitutes a case of cultural colonization with a Western code of signification. As a result, the East is always represented, even in its representation of the West. The East is spoken instead of speaking, for lack of its own language to express itself. Consequently, the East has no way to write its own history except to be a text colonized in terms of the West, for the West.

If Marxism functions as the first powerful negation of Chinese history, culture and society in the modern era, China is facing the second challenge of the West after the forbidden gate has opened to end the age of voyeurism and the Cold War. The authoritative voice of Marxism functioning as the metanarrative of history is gradually losing its traditional privilege as universal truth and is diminishing its power over the motion of history in China. Since 1980, China has made tremendous effort to modernize itself in every aspect: economic structure, industrial management, education system, moral values, lifestyle and cultural tradition. Basically it is considered a silent revolution, an intentional Westward movement. Historical r/evolution or not, it is inevitably a process of collision between the new West (characterized by technology and democracy) and the old West (characterized by utopianism and classes). With the entrance of the current Western culture, there has been a temporary revival of traditional Chinese cultural heritages, mainly Confucianism and Taoism, to meet the challenge. It is evident that China's future depends on the collision of these three historical and cultural powers: the old Western Marxism (a form of European romanticism), the new Western materialism (a form of American pragmatism), and the Eastern Confucianism and Taoism. Some people hold a nostalgic view, lamenting the loss of history in the future; whereas others are eager to project the future of a capitalist China with a real bourgeois class emerging on native soil. Is this a return or eternal return? And who can tell? Who can tell the direction of history (whose history)? Who can say that history is not a process of displacement, and a makeup of history? From this point of view, history is not something to be returned to, or to be kept, but something to be invented.

It seems irreversible that Marxism as a masternarrative of history is going to be displaced by new Western ideas after it has possessed China for half a century. Socialist China is giving in to capitalist penetration, confusingly, resistingly and hesitatingly. This process meets with constant setbacks and at tremendous cost. The Tian An Men Square massacre of June 4 1989 is but a prelude to the major note of the displacement of Marxism. On a limited scale, private ownership is displacing public ownership, and foreign investment is taking the place of self-reliance. The state-planned economy is giving way to a free market economy. As a result, socialism is being dissolved materially by capitalist materialism, and the whole content of socialism is being deflated and evacuated into an empty signifier of nothing or anything. Marxism exists only in name and remains a name in China. Since the 1980's, China has been substituting the term commercialism for capitalism, as a less threatening term (not only economically, but historically). China wants to confront the real West, not the West displaced in Marxist textbooks. Thousands of students from mainland China have come to Europe and America (myself included), to re-educate themselves with Western knowledge and Western culture. Voyeurism has given way to free play with the Western body. China's future is not difficult to predict: displacement is inevitable in the Westward movement.

From a postmodern position, the history of China, or rather histories of China, can be regarded as a process of dissociation, fragmentation and discontinuity. As history is dispersed into histories, we are at a loss to construct a coherent narrative of history with continuity. Which represents the true China: Hongkong, Taiwan or mainland China? None of them can claim that "it" represents China without referring to the fact of displacement. All of them have undergone the process of Westernization, although at different historical points and after different models. Hence, Chinese history is split into three different simultaneous processes under the power of the West: socialism in mainland China developed by communists after the model of Marxism via the Russian revolution, which places Marxism in an ambiguous territory of neither East nor West; capitalism developed in Taiwan by nationalists after the model of America; and colonialism developed in Hongkong after the model of Great Britain. Finally, who represents the true face (not to say essence) of China in modern history? If Chinese history is under construction, then by whom?

The ten-year cultural revolution in China is more than an anecdote. Millions of people died for it, either actively or passively, victimizers or victimized. A whole generation of the cultural revolution suicidally struggled, not with the substance of the other (the bourgeois), but with a mere shadow of the self they were not allowed to possess. They died because of a mistake of translation and displacement. They tried their best to eradicate a bourgeois class consciousness which did not exist at all. Finally their energy, aroused for destruction, turned inward. They had to purify their own bodies by castrating their desires through constant self-criticism. Any possibility of any authentic self had been negated to the point of abolition, the abolition of consciousness and subjectivity. Nothing is more tragic in human history than a whole generation denied the right to possess individuality and consciousness.

Fascism is a product of ideology. Internationally, ideology accounts for several historical disasters. The McCarthyism of America during the 1950's, when the anti-communist movement intensified on a national scale, now has become a classroom joke (the American way to history). The Anti-Trotsky movement in the Soviet Union, when millions of people were executed and persecuted, is merely considered a historical mistake. And the cultural revolution in China. All these political and ideological movements have been conducted according to the two dominant signifiers of ideology — communism and capitalism, the forms of history deformed by historical materialism, and the binary positions of structural theory overdetermined in a Hegelian dialectics.

This essay is indebted to all the victims of displaced history, essentially to the lost generation of the cultural revolution, for their mistakes, and our awakening, but not the awakening of class consciousness. In confrontation with the new challenge of the West, the younger generation of China has to seek an independent "we" of life, and a history that is not displaced.

I apologize for having written this "recollection" in another tongue and on the other side of China, in a postmodern stance toward history. I have committed the very sin I have blamed on the subject of this essay. Irony is the only idiom of my existence.

Cezar Ornatowski

The "Government of the Tongue":
Eloquence and Subjection
in Renaissance Rhetorical Theory

> Bar. I have no tongue, Sir.
>
> Page. And as for mine, Sir, I will govern it.
>
> (*2 Henry IV* IV, ii, 160)

IN A STRIKING EPISODE IN BOOK V of the *Faerie Queene* Arthur and Artegall enter the castle of Mercilla led by Order, marshall of the hall, and behold "Some one whose tongue was for his trespass vyle/ Nayld to a post, adiudged so by law." Above the penitent's head are the words "Bon Font," but "Bon" has been "raced out" and "Mal" written in, so that now "Malfont was plainly to be read;/ Eyther for th'evill, which he did therein,/ Or that he likened was to a welhed/ Of evill words/ (*FQ* Book V Canto IX).

In the "penal semiotics" of the spectacle of Bon/Malfont's punishment, the tongue "nayled to a post" is the focal object and the site of the application of power. It is neutralized, immobilized, and exposed to public view in a variation of pillorying. Pillorying was typically associated with moral trespasses, trespasses that threatened the sustaining values of the community. It was a common punishment for cheating (for instance, for false measure), for immorality, for offenses against religion, and for seditious speech. It is of this last offence that Bon/Malfont is presumably guilty, since he "falsely did revyle,/ And foule blaspheme" his queen.

As a literary spectacle, the scene depends, like the public spectacle it reenacts, on what Foucault has called a "technology of representation," the creation of a complex sign that sets in motion "a play of representations and signs circulating discreetly but necessarily in the minds of all".[1] The scene at once communicates, reinforces, and draws its meaning from the audience's realization of that to which it testifies: the dual truth of the power of language and the power of the queen to

---

[1] Michel Foucault, *Discipline and Punish*, trans. Alan Sheridan, (New York: Vintage, 1979), p. 101.

control it. Its "play of representations and signs" suggests that language constitutes, on the one hand, one of the sources ("font") of power and, on the other hand, an object of its application and a means of its exercise. It also suggests a complex set of representations of the relationship between language, social order, and rule, representations from which the spectacle of Bon/Malfont's punishment derives its sense and which it (re)awakens and sets in motion to "circulate discreetly in the minds of all."

It is these representations that I wish to examine in the present paper. These representations, I will argue, underlie Renaissance prescriptions for the conduct of speech and the assumptions about what Louis Montrose has called "the relationship between the verbal and the social"[2] that stand behind the commonplace association — repeatedly asserted in Renaissance rhetorics — of eloquent speech with social order.

The insistence with which Renaissance rhetorics assert the connection between eloquence and social order has led Brian Vickers to suggest that "the connection between speech, reason, and order [...] is basic to English sixteenth century thinking about language".[3] This connection is usually explained, both by Renaissance rhetoricians as well as by modern scholars, in terms of the persuasive power of speech. Vickers, for instance, suggests that "rhetoric not only produces or organizes speech as expression, but above all things it controls speech for persuasion".[4] Whigham, similarly to Vickers, argues that rhetoric "maintains rule by persuading subjects to submit."[5] This interpretation has been widely accepted since it appears entirely consistent with the classical sources of Renaissance rhetorical theory in Plato, Aristotle, Cicero, and Quintilian, as well as with its more immediate sources in the writings of Erasmus, Aphthonius, or Susenbrotus.

In my analysis, however, I want to approach the problem of the relationship between language and social order from another angle altogether. Rather than attempt to account for the illocutionary power of rhetoric, as the source of its effectiveness, I will try to reconstruct the commonplace (in the sense of rhetorical "commonplaces" or tropes) representations of the relationship between speech (language) and social order — the correspondences, homologies, and transformations in terms of which that relationship was constructed and thought — representations that rendered scenes such as that of Bon/Malfont's punishment

---

[2] Louis Montrose, "Professing the Renaissance: The Poetics and Politics of Culture," in: H. Aram Veeser, *The New Historicism*, (London: Routledge, 1989), p. 23.

[3] Brian Vickers, "The Power of Persuasion Images of the Orator, Elyot to Shakespeare." In James J. Murphy, *Renaissance Eloquence: Studies in the Theory and Practice of Renaissance Rhetoric*, (Berkeley: University of California Press, 1983), p. 416.

[4] Ibidem, p. 417.

[5] Frank Whigham, *Ambition and Privilege: Social Tropes of Elizabethan Courtesy Theory*, (Berkeley: U of California Press, 1984), p. 2.

politically intelligible and poetically potent. I will also argue, that such representations underlie Renaissance rhetorical prescriptions and that it is in these
representations, rather then in an appeal to a generalized persuasive power of
rhetoric, that the political effectiveness of these prescriptions — and the political
project of Renaissance rhetoric — ought to be located.

In a treatise "A Direction for the Government of the Tongue According to
Gods Word" (1600), William Perkins, a Protestant preacher, educator, and
occasional rhetorician, outlines a political anatomy of the body, with a focus on
the "tongue."[6] According to this anatomy,

> The minde is the guide of the tongue: therefore men must consider before they
> speake. The tongue is the messenger of the heart, and therefore as oft as we
> speake without meditation going before, so oft the messenger runneth without his
> errand. The tongue is placed in the middle of the mouth, and it is compassed in
> with lips and teeth as with a double trench, to showe us, howe we are to use
> heede and preconsideration before we speake: and therefore it is good advise, to
> keep the key of the mouth not in the mouth but in the cupboard of the mouth.
> Augustine saith well, that as in eating and drinking men make choice of meates:
> so in manifolde speeches we should make choice of talke.[7]

The "tongue" emerges here as the central organ, both in terms of its instrumental
importance and of its positioning in the "anatomy" that is marshalled to reinforce
the argument for the necessity of its control. Since the heart is the fountain of
speech, for the "right ordering" of speech "the pure heart is most necessary,"
because "if the fountaine be defiled, the streames that issue thence can not be
cleane." However, "because the heart of man by nature is a bottomlesse gulfe of
iniquitie, two things are to be knowne: first, how it must be made pure: & then
how it is alwayes afterward to be kept pure."[8] Both, according to Perkins, are
achieved through "government of the tongue."

In Perkins's scheme, the "government of the tongue" is the foundation for a
discipline of affects through which one's corrupt nature is purified. Through its
reciprocal connection with the mind and the heart, the "tongue" emerges as both
a symptom and an instrument of "right ordering." Through a common Renaissance
homology between "microcosm" and "macrocosm," the self and the commonwealth, the "tongue" serves also as the symptom and the instrument of both
personal and collective right ordering. In Perkin's political anatomy, the "tongue"
thus occupies the central place as at once a powerful moral and political weapon,
a double-edged sword that unites the individual and the body politic through its

---

[6] William Perkins, "A Direction for the Government of the Tongue According to Gods Word."
A Golden Chain, (Cambridge, 1600), p. 712–734; (Anne Arbor: University Microfilms, 1968).

[7] Ibidem, p. 716.

[8] Ibidem, p. 713.

capacity as a gauge and an instrument of, on the one hand, moral ordering in the personal sphere and, on the other hand, of public order.

It is worth noting, at this point, that Perkins's "government of the tongue" does not consist of persuasive employment of speech, much less of a persuasive intent aimed at others. Its is, rather, a form of self-control that simultaneously represents an opening for external control. The connection between speech and social order that the term implies is not that of cause and effect; it is, rather, of the order of a form of presence of social structures in a set of linguistic practices.

A similar set of representations emerges from an examination of the Renaissance senses of "government of the tongue" and of "government" itself. The *OED* records two popular Renaissance meanings for the "government of the tongue": holding in check, curbing, bridling, as well as regulation and control. Sir Philip Sidney used a semantic variant of it when in the *Old Arcadia* he called Fame the "governour of many tongues." For "govern," on the other hand, the *OED* records ten different sixteenth century meanings. They include: to regulate in action or motives, to influence or sway, to determine the course or issue, to conduct oneself, to behave oneself properly, to order (as arrange, put in order), to attend to, to look after, to watch, to manipulate, to hold in check or to curb, to constitute a law or rule, to control or regulate the working of a machine, to tend or treat in respect to health, and to key a musical instrument (in the sense of tuning to a dominant sound).

The most notable departures from modern usage cluster around regulation and coordination of mechanical operations or physical quantities; imposition of regularity, order, and comprehensible patterning; and, most importantly perhaps, the "reversibility" of control: control from "within" (self-control) as well as control "from without" (control of others). This last pair of connotations also includes control in the sense of physiological regulation and care of the body.

In sixteenth century English, "government" thus encompasses the whole semantic cluster of control and repression, including mechanical control, psychological and physiological manipulation, imposition of order, and making comprehensible (and thus rulable) what would otherwise remain chaotic and obscure (and thus misruled). This semantic cluster of "ordering" (and the associated connotation of rulability) applies both to the self and to the "body politic."

Like Greenblatt's "self-fashioning," self-control in the use of speech is both a kind of "power to impose a shape upon oneself" as well as an "aspect of the more general power to control identity — that of others at least as much as one's own."[9] In Perkin's anatomy, the "tongue" is the bridge between the individual body and the social-political body. The linguistic self-discipline through which,

[9] Stephen Greenblatt, *Renaissance Self-Fashioning: From More to Shakespeare*, (Chicago: U of Chicago Press, 1980), p. 1.

according to Perkins's argument, one's own self is transformed and "ordered," that is rendered *rulable*, is also a powerful instrument of ordering (and ruling) other selves — no less so because it is also a symptom of both individual and collective moral health, and thus constitutes a check as well as a means of surveillance and control. This double opening of the "government" performed by the tongue is semantically expressed in its equivocation between self-control and being controlled, between speaking and "being spoken." Control of one's own tongue becomes at once a condition for effective action and a modality of subjectification, an instrument of control and an opening for being controlled.

The exploitation of this ambiguity is perhaps the political project — Mercilla's as well as Spenser's — behind the spectacle of Bon/Malfont. On the one hand, while Mercilla's purpose is to inscribe her authority on the organ that unites her subjects into a community that is the state (*her* state), Spenser draws attention to the fact that it is indeed that organ (not only Bon/Malfont's tongue but his own as the author of the *Fearie Queene*) that to a large extent also authorizes her power to do so, as well as defines its limits and puts it in question. As Montrose has suggested, Spenser's project in the *Fearie Queene* is perhaps "to put into question [authority's] absolute claims upon the subjects who produce the forms in which it authorizes itself," since in the process of inscription, "the subject is in some very limited but nevertheless quite real sense also constituting the sovereignty in relation to which his own subjection and his subjectivity are constituted."[10]

On the other hand, the "tongue" serves Mercilla both as a gauge of the political health of the commonwealth and of her subjects' loyalty (just as for Perkins it was a gauge of their spiritual/moral health) as well as an instrument of control. Her mutilation of Bon/Malfont therefore marks out one end of the spectrum of political possibilities opened up by the representation of the relationship between speech, social order, and rule implied in the notion of "government of the tongue." Its other end emerges from Perkins's apocalyptic vision of a "man with an ungoverned tongue":

> The man of an evil tongue, is a beast in the forme of a man; for his tongue is the tongue of a serpent, under which lieth nothing but venom and poison: nay he is worse than a serpent: for it cannot hurte, unlesse it bee present to see a man, or to bite him or to strike him with his taile: but he which hath not the rule of his tongue, hurteth men as well absent as present, neither sea nor land, not any thing can hinder him. And againe, his throat is like a grave that hath a vent in some part, and therefore sendeth forth nothing but stink and corruption. III. As the holy men of God when they preached, had their tongues, as it were, touched with

[10] Louis A. Montrose, "The Elizabethan Subject and the Spenserian Text." in: Patricia Parker and David Quint, *Literary Theory/Renaissance Texts*, (Baltimore and London: The Johns Hopkins UP, 1986), p. 33 f.

a cole from the altar of God: and as godly men when they speak graciously, have their tongues inflamed with the fire of Gods spirit: so contrariwise, when thou speaketh evill, thy tongue is kindled by the fire of hell and Sathan comes from thence with a cole to touch thy lipps, and to set them on fire to all manner of mischiefe.[11]

The vision of the man with an ungoverned tongue as the "beast in the forme of a man" allied with the devil and ready to commit "all manner of mischiefe" points out the convergence between the interests of the ruler and the interests of the subjects: if speech is the instrument and guarantor of "civilization," if it is that which separates humanity from "beastliness," its control becomes not only a private and moral concern but a political necessity of government as well.

The "tongue" thus becomes a sign that marks the mutuality of interests between the ruler and the ruled. Its control serves, paradoxically, as a confirmation of this mutuality and a guarantor and condition of "civil" government. The spectacle of Bon/Malfont's punishment ultimately constitutes, for Spenser as well as for the Spenserian reader (and the primary addressed reader of the *Faerie Queene* is of course Elizabeth herself), not a subversive representation of royal abuse but a confirmation and celebration — through the play of signs and representations which it sets in motion "to circulate discreetly in the minds of all" — of civic and divine order and a confirmation that the interests of the governed are identical with the interests of the body politic and the interests of the queen.

The political project of English Renaissance rhetoric was, in general, to provide rhetorical forms that could serve as appropriate avenues for the exchange of mutual interests within such a conception of civic order. The general principles of this exchange are most clearly expressed in Guazzo's treatise *Civile Conversation*, popular in England in George Petti's translation.[12]

Guazzo's Count Annibale begins by arguing for the necessity of engaging in interpersonal relations ("conversation"). "Conversation," declares Annibale, "is the beginning and end of knowledge."[13] Therefore, "as the trueth is taken from the common consent and opinion of men, those opinions cannot be knowen but by conversation and companie."[14] Participation in "conversation" is thus necessary "to get wisedome, to come by the accomplishment of learning, and to come to dignitie, riches, and worldly promotions."[15] "Conversation" means here, of course, not only verbal exchange; its full meaning in the Renaissance included

---

[11] William Perkins, op. cit., p. 732 f.

[12] Stephano Guazzo, *Civile Conversatione*. Trans. George Petti, repr. (New York: AMF Press, 1967).

[13] Ibidem, p. 39.

[14] Ibidem, p. 41.

[15] Ibidem, p. 46.

relating to others, intercourse (including sexual intercourse), society, as well as the manner of conducting oneself, behaviour, mode and course of life. Thus, when Annibale declares that "civile conversation is an honest, commendable, and virtuous living in the world,"[16] he is declaring that relating to others in a manner to be defined as "civil" is an essential element of socially-approved manner of living.

But "conversation" does not simply mean any "relation"; it denotes, rather, a fundamentally social relation, that is, a relation not between individuals but between social "sites." As such, "conversation" appears to be defined in the *Civile Conversation* as an exchange of the duties and responsibilities that inhere in each social position in regard to the other. The rules of "conversation" are a function of the mutual social positioning of participants. That is apparent in Annibale's grouping of social relations into representative categories before prescribing the "manner of conversation" that should obtain within each. For instance, while laying down the rules for "domesticall conversation, that is to say, within the house," he groups all possible relations that regularly occur between members of a household into the following pairs: Husband-Wife, Father-Son, Brother-Brother, and Master-Servant.

It is important to note, however, that in this scheme designations such as "Father," "Master," "Brother," and "Servant" represent not individuals or types but abstract sites which subsume all members of a household who share analogous duties and responsibilities towards other members. Thus, the category of "Father" subsumes also "Tutor," "Uncle," and "Father in Law," while the category "Master" subsumes "Mistress," etc. In this strongly "structuralist" scheme, the social system (in the present example the localized micro-system of the household) is represented as a network of loci or sites defined not in relation to their occupants but mainly in terms of their mutual orientation: in terms of what is "due" from and to each. Thus, "Father" designates the site of authority in relation to a site such as "Son." The mother as a figure of authority in relation to the daughter falls therefore into the site of "Father." However, in relation to "Husband" the mother is reclassified into the site of "Wife," since her duties and responsibilities within the Husband-Wife relationship are different from what they were in relation to the daughter.

The mutual duties and responsibilities are expressed both verbally and through behaviour, both of which comprise "conversation." In the most general sense, then, Guazzo's "civile conversation" designates behaviour which provides the most convenient means for an exchange of the mutual "dues" inhering in the social sites occupied by the interlocutors. The tacit understanding of this enables Guazzo to exclaim, after Annibale explains the responsibilities of the father towards the son,

---

[16] Ibidem, p 56.

"by the discourse already made, I have partly learned, how the father ought to behave himself towards the childe."[17] It is also this assumption that lies behind Annibale' answer, after Guazzo requests that Annibale explain to him the "duty of the childe" towards the father, "If the childe consider well the great and extreme love of the father towards him, there should neede no forme of conversation to be prescribed onto him, for that consideration would containe him in his duty, and make him conforme himselfe to the will and pleasure of his father, in all thinges."[18]

That the desirable "manner of conversation" is indeed grounded in the totality of presuppositions that define a given social position is apparent when Guazzo and Annibale, in discussing the proper conduct of "conversation" between a gentleman and a yeoman begin by trying to define what constitutes gentility, what makes a yeoman, and what is the "nature" of the social distinction between the two.[19] Henry Peacham, in his *The Complete Gentleman*, similarly mixes prescriptions for how a gentleman should conduct himself in speech with reflections on the origins and nature of nobility and on the duties and responsibilities of a gentleman.

The prescriptions for verbal conduct that emerge from the *Civile Conversation* cast the structure of the social system in rhetorical terms. In these terms, speech emerges as less a means of "communication" than an integral element of social positioning: an articulation of a social position through and in relation to other positions that form the social network. Thus, each socially contextualized use of speech expresses, in large part, the social relation between interlocutors and is couched in the totality of presuppositions which surround their social positions. Each use of speech is also an expression of socially sanctioned self-images, self-presentations, and representations of the "other" consistent with the social position occupied by a speaker in relation to the position of the interlocutor.[20]

The ultimate goal of Guazzo's prescriptions for "civil conversation" is to promote social harmony, prevent discord, and maintain established social relations. The general progression of the discussion is "First, [...] [to] show the occasion of the discorde and inconveniences which arise every day amongst [parties in 'conversation,' in the particular context between masters and servants], and afterwards [...] seeke the meane to make all well, and to agree them together."[21] This "meane" is the rhetorical prescriptions for the conduct of civil conversation. The avowed purpose of such prescriptions is to "set downe some such order that

[17] Ibidem, B. III, p. 69.

[18] Ibidem, B. III, p. 71.

[19] Ibidem, Book II, p. 174 f.

[20] It is in this sense perhaps that Norbert Elias has suggested that "speech is nothing other than social relations turned into sound." (*History of Manners*, vol. 1, p. 117).

[21] Ibidem, B. III, p. 96.

the Mayster and the servant may lyve and continue long time quietly together,"[22] and they accomplish it by prescribing to each the proper manner of discharging their social obligations. Thus, to the master they prescribe the proper "manner of commaunding," while to the servant they prescribe the proper manner of obeying.

Daniel Tuvill, an essayist active at the beginning of the seventeenth century, in his essay "Of Civill Carriage and Conversation," suggests that the "civill" speaker must "beware of everything that may cause either friction or division [...]."[23] "Man is like onto a bee," he explains in the opening of the essay, "for whereas other creatures do no sooner come into the world but that are able of their own proper strength to raise themselves upon their feet, he alone hath need of outward aid and assistance." The faculty of speech comes in therefore "to the end that he might confer and negotiate with those of his own kind and not be any way defective in the performance of such offices as are necessarily required for the preservation of human society."[24] One of Puttenham's notorious anecdotes in the *Arte* recounts a defective performance of such an office. An intercessor for "one Sir Anthony Rouse" asked King Henry VIII to remember the said Rouse "with some reward for that he had spent much and was an ill beggar: the king answered, (noting his insolencie,) If he be ashamed to begge, we are ashamed to give."[25] Rouse's "insolencie" consists in the implicit refusal to participate in an exchange in which his status as subject and the king's status as the sovereign could be rehearsed and confirmed by their respective roles of petitioner and grantor.

Whigham has noted the importance of such ritual exchanges in his analysis of the letters of Elizabethan suitors to their patrons. The suitor, says Whigham, "understood the force of imposing on the patron a mantle of generosity, the refusal of which disconfirmed the *patron's* status, not the petitioner's."[26] He concludes that in the polite formulas of assuring the interlocutor of one's gratitude and obligation the "ability to perform services [...] matters less than the public ratification of station" provided by such assurances.

Rouse's transgression, therefore, lies in his failure to reenact the required spectacle of supplication and reward that would confirm both him and the king in their political roles. As Puttenham explains it,

---

[22] Ibidem, B. III, p. 104.

[23] Daniel Tuvill, *Essays Politic and Moral and Essays Moral and Theological*. Ed. John Lievsay. Folger Documents in Tudor and Stuart Civilisation, (Charlotteville: The University Press of Virginia, 1971), p. 89.

[24] Ibidem, p. 87.

[25] George Puttenham, *The Arte of Anglish Poesie*, Kent English Reprints: The Renaissance, (The Kent State University Press, 1970). p. 301.

[26] Frank Whigham, "The Rhetoric of Elizabethan Suitors' Letters," *PLMA* 96 (1981), p. 874.

in a Prince it is comely to give unasked, but in a subject to ask unbidden: for the first is a signe of a bountifull mynde, this of a loyall and confident. But the subject that craves not at his Princes hand either he is of no desert, or proud, or mistrustfull of his Princes goodnesse.[27]

"Craving at the prince's hand" becomes an occasion for both participants in the exchange to rehearse their respective social roles: to the subject, it is an occasion to express allegiance and trust; to the king, it is an opportunity to show generosity and to exercise one of the major prerogatives and symbols of rule: the granting of bounty.[28] The act of social interaction — in this case suing for favours — is thus not only a private gesture performed for personal ends but a political act through which social positions and structures are defined, clarified, authorized, and perpetuated. Each such act constitutes a link in the chain of relations that links subject and sovereign. The story illustrates the reciprocal and instrumental relationship between a form or ritual through which rule is discharged and upheld and rhetorical prescriptions whose function turns out to be indeed to assist in the performance of "such offices as are necessarily required for the preservation of human society."[29] It is through the proper performance of such rituals that the commonwealth is ordered and, in the Renaissance corollary of the term, rendered rulable.

As the Rouse story shows, however, such "offices" did not always get performed correctly; Rouse would have the rewards of the system (through an intermediary) without doing his share in upholding it. It is the sort of breakdown in the social-political machinery that, quite apart from the persuasive potential of eloquence, may have prompted Peacham's exhortation to rulers to maintain "honest and eloquent orators [...] near about them as no mean props, if occasion serve, to uphold a state, and the only keys to bring in tune a discordant commonwealth."[30]

Marc Fumaroli has suggested that the centrality of rhetoric in the Renaissance is a product of the specific nature of "civil" society: that "what we call the Renaissance was, among other fundamental characteristics, the affirmation in itself [...] of a civil society, distinct in its very finality from religious and military society [...]."[31] Rhetoric, Fumaroli suggests, assumed the role of "the connective tissue peculiar to civil society and to its proper finalities, happiness and political

---

[27] George Puttenham, *The Arte of English Poesie*, op. cit., p. 301.

[28] The specific mechanisms involved in the use of royal favours as a form of rule have been described by Norbert Elias, *The Court Society*, (New York: Pantheon, 1983).

[29] Daniel Tuvill, op. cit., p. 87.

[30] Henry Peacham, *The Complete Gentleman*, op. cit., p. 18.

[31] Marc Fumaroli, "Rhetoric, Politics, and Society: From Italian Ciceronianism to French Classicism," in James J. Murphy, *Renaissance Eloquence*, op. cit., p. 253.

peace hic et nunc."[32] The "government of the tongue" provides a way of thinking this "connectivity" simultaneously in political and rhetorical terms: in those terms, the political project of Renaissance rhetoric in general was an elaboration of a detailed code of verbal (self)control that ensured social unity and provided legitimation for centralized rule and for the social system while providing avenues through which this rule could be discharged, mutual interests could be negotiated, and the system could function and perpetuate itself with a minimum of friction.

This project represents perhaps a response to what Whigham has called the "rule of words" in early modern Europe. Whigham ascribes the ascendancy of rhetoric to the increasing centralization and bureaucratization of the early-modern state, in which "the combative chivalric ideology of moralized force was altered by new cooperative pressures of nationally centralized life."[33] In the new social and political configuration, "problems of power once solved by force were now submitted to a *rule of words*."[34] The semantic ambiguities implicit in the phrase "rule of words": ruling versus being ruled through words, the agency of speakers versus their subjection to the rules and forms of verbal interaction, reflect, as I have tried to show, the ambiguous and reflexive relationship between language, social order, and rule implicit strongly in the notion of "government of the tongue." The set of practices that constitute this "government" may be taken to represent a specific and characteristic application of general rhetorical principles in social practice. In these practices, rhetoric emerges as at once an art of conduct, a technology of the body (especially with the development of the art of elocution), and an important, if not central, instrument of rule.

Rhetorical prescriptions regulated interaction across the social spectrum, between genders, classes, estates, and degrees: between husbands and wives, masters and servants, patrons and suitors, and fathers and sons. Through the coordinates of decorum, these prescriptions conditioned routine expectations and responses towards people and situations and contributed to one's sense of place in the social field and one's conception of self as reflected in the dynamics of social interaction. Ultimately, they served to interrelate "private" and "public" functions and allowed social personae to be represented in and to adapt to the political and social systems, granting the means of engagement in and response to the rituals through which the social order was expressed and maintained. They thus constitute one of the major modalities of "subjectification," that "equivocal process" that Louis Montrose has described as

> on the one hand, shaping individuals as loci of consciousness and initiators of action — endowing them with *subjectivity* and with the capacity for agency; and

---

[32] Ibidem, p. 253.

[33] Frank Whigham, *Ambition and Privilege*, op. cit., p. 13.

[34] Ibidem; Whigham's emphasis.

on the other hand, positioning, motivating, and constraining them within —
subjecting them to — social networks and cultural codes that ultimately exceed
their comprehension or control.[35]

This dual thrust of subjectification, reflected in the semantic ambiguity of the term
"subject" itself, which, as Montrose points out, is a "simultaneously grammatical
and political term" (an ambiguity especially appropriate in the present context),
situates the subject at the nexus of the linguistic "ordering" that, as Perkins has
argued, reaches on the one hand, into human "nature" and on the other hand,
towards the commonwealth. This ordering defines to a large extent the possibilities
of individual agency in the social context as well as grounds social and political
structures in linguistic practices. It is these tasks that constitute the political
project of Renaissance rhetoric and it is the machinery of representations employed to support them, rather than the power of persuasion per se, that are the
means through which rhetoric "maintains rule."[36]

[35] Louis Montrose, "Professing the Renaissance," op. cit., p. 21.

[36] Frank Whigham, *Ambition and Privilege*, op. cit., p. 2.

Kenneth Mendoza

Recovering Presence

CURRENT STUDY OF ORAL POETICS and Native American literature demonstrates the inadequacy and distortion associated when expression of a complex multi-faceted cultural literature is conformed and translated into familiar categories of literate western culture. The insistence of our literary conditioned analysis for one-to-one correspondence identifies the limits of the literate Western focus and analysis rather than revealing the artistic activity and diversity of "theirs." Although the most basic characteristic of oral poetics — actual performances — is no mystery, this feature is rarely transported into our purview when critically analyzing the literature. Oral poets perform, formulating words, dance, and music on disparate occasions. Searching analytically to explain and translate the phenomena of oral performances leads us deep into the wastelands of our own cultural disposition which now needs liberating. What can be learned about oral poetic expression will not only enlarge our understanding of our tribal pasts, but also reveal our present: offering our Western critical tradition, one rooted in the clearly delineated analytic text, an expanded dimension for expressive possibilities.

Oral poetry redefines the limits of the text and extends literary expression to the living plane. It draws on performance — on dancing, singing, pantomime, and music — and very little on the expressive techniques we commonly associate with poetic expression in cultures of a Western literary orientation. Oral poetry involves a performance manifold which develops not from the focus of Western psychological theater (an attitude dominating Western poetic expression, largely dependent on a verbally expressed conflict of feelings), but rather states perceptions of the mind, crystallized and articulated through a language of analogies. Every component in oral poetry is designed and charged with value: the vehicle which drives this art to life is the complex abundance of all the stratagems of the performance which impose on our minds a metaphysics derived from the utilization of gesture and voice.

Oral poetic performance executes what may be characterized as "pure" theater: every concept and realization has value or exists in terms of the total dimensions of performance, where the language of gesture eliminates words and presents images. The amalgamated language expressing oral art encompasses the variables of modulated vocables erupting from the recesses of the throat, the shaking of rattles, the pounding of drums, sudden and impudent rhythms, animated dances, and abruptly shifting postures, which gather to emerge and define a physical language grounded in gesture rather than words. The language of oral poetry has precise meaning which strike and direct us intuitively and which renders useless any critic's attempt to reduce this expression into logical discursive language reflecting the Western aesthetic palate.

> We Sioux spend a lot of time thinking about everyday things which in our mind are mixed up with the spiritual. We see in the world around us many symbols that teach us the meaning of life. We have a saying that the white man sees so little, he must see with only one eye. We see a lot that you no longer notice. You could notice if you wanted to, but you are usually to busy. We Indians live in a world of symbols and images where spiritual and commonplace are one. To you symbols are just words, spoken or written in a book. To us they are part of nature, part of ourselves — the earth, the sun, the wind and the rain, stones, trees, animals, even the little insects like ants and grasshoppers. We try to understand them not with the head but with the heart, and we need no more than a hint to give us the meaning [...]. What to you seems commonplace to us appears wondrous through symbolism. This is funny, because we don't even have a word for symbolism, yet we are all wrapped up in it. You have the word, but that is all.[1]

The participants of oral performance lose their identities behind the illusion that oral poetic language creates. Performers assume a double — an artistic persona — who translates imaginary apparition into concrete image. The cries of vocables, the dance-foot rhythmically striking the earth and raising dust, the song and music being released into the air acts upon and liberates our unconscious, offering us an image extending to realism — reflecting and re-enforcing the perceptual act of living. We confront our concrete selves and not some vaguely defined outline posited by an apparitional performer. The repertoire of gestures correspond and clarify the circumstance of living; every action, movement, sound, and word develops into a spiritual architecture, constructed not only of gestures and sign language, but also of the evocational power of rhythm, the musical quality of physical movement and the harmony of discordant sounds. This assault on our senses, pouring toward, extending to, and incorporating audience may challenge and startle Western sensibilities of literary and theatrical conventions, yet the product of this offering has an undeniable impact resulting from the image this literature sparks. The constant fusion of elements uniting sight with sound, intellect with sensibility, the gesture of performer maneuvering beside a suggestive movement of a ray of sunlight; all this synergistic energy overlaid across the cry of a voice or a shrill whistle establishes an architecture of the metaphysics of form. The pitch of the musical instrument acts to sustain the cry of a voice, blending the two to such an extent that an analogy is established, and

---

[1] John Fire and Lame Deer, "The Circle and the Square," *Literatures of the American Indians: Views and Interpretations*, (New York: New American Library, 1975), p. 78.

differentiating between them is impossible. The expression becomes a perpetual play of forces reinforcing and mimicking perception while simultaneously reinforcing image.

> Everything in the spiritual realm as well as the natural, is significant, reciprocal, correspondent [...] everything is hieroglyphic [...] and the poet is merely the translator, the one who deciphers.[2]

The range and dimensions of oral poetic expression obviously cannot be approached from a Western mode of literary analysis. The dialectic gestured language of oral poetry abound with a multitude of impressions and meanings which directs our awareness to acts and language we no longer possess. Gary Snyder described to me a very special literary moment he experienced while observing a Native American performer re-enacting a Bear Dance. This particular performance became very special "when the dancer became the bear" and was "not a dancer, dancing like a bear." The poetic event for participant and audience extended the arena of stage and became "real" and "live" at the moment of aesthetic realization. Obviously Snyder's delight and declarative observations test the tethers of Western sensibility and we would prefer to assume that Snyder's language as merely figurative. The inability (or unwillingness) of Western scholarship to identify and acknowledge these artistic moments perhaps only affirms and reveals the beauty of this art. Expression is not confined to an idiom comprehended only upon hearing, but rather becomes a language which is external to spoken language and extends to the experience beyond the stage of performance. The expressive language acquired from this extended stage demands that as audience, we treat the events of performance as actual living conditions, and we ourselves become performers in the kinetic events. Western poetic and theatrical productions focusing exclusively on psychological dialogue establish a performance stage that limits the associative exchange between audience and stage. The audience assumes the posture of voyeur through a proscenium window, subject to the restrictive boundaries of a text designed with a premeditated static resolve.

> The objects which occur at any given moment of composition [...] are, can be, must be treated exactly as they do occur therein and not by any ideas or preconceptions from outside the poem [...] must be handled as a series of objects in field [...] a series of tensions [...] space-tensions of a poem [...] the acting-on-you of the poem.[3]

The same elements which characterize oral poetic expression challenge our Western conceptions of poetry and literature; applying *our* analysis to this oral

---

[2] Charles Baudelaire, *L'Art romantique*, ed. Jaques Crépet, (Paris: Conrad, 1925), p. 507.

[3] Olsen and Creeley, "Projected Verse", *Poetry New York*, No. 3 (1950); also in: Charles Olson, *Selected Writings*, (New York: New Directions, 1966), p. 20.

expression would endanger our discovering the quality of this poetry. We find the constituents of this expression disconcerting; Western scholarship tends to separate the fabric of oral poetry placing emphasis on a text which may be reduced to logical discursive language. Oral poetry utilizes a language of another caste, a language of ritual gestures, and a language that we have *no* difficulty deciphering if approached from outside our critical-analytic agendas. This language is closely associated with musical designations, yet its focus does not belong to music, but rather pursues the articulation of a thought-image outside of sound, verbal language, and movement. Every aspect of the performance sustains an equilibrium: the song erupting from the throat; instruments and environment transfuse with the sonorous joining of the physical movements of dance, mime and natural forces; eliminating transition, all elements culminating in the crystallization of an image/thought.

The actions, movements, and expressions of oral poets do not seem to belong to themselves, but embody and obey established languages that reflect other concerns and intelligences. The poets assume the double, an effigy of themselves, becoming living hieroglyphs. The intensity of the ceremonial event possesses the capacity to extend our perceptions to a point where phenomena is entertained. Western performance drama, focusing almost exclusively on dialogue, lacks this phenomenological potential. For instance, the specific intention of an oral poet may be to direct our attention into isolating and capturing the sound of morning light. For the poet, the actions involved in producing sounds are established through a dynamic that relies upon physically executed gesture that qualifies the quality of sound. Through the association of sound and gesture, a musical analogy is established. We synthesize the articulated gesture of movement with the resonance of sound rendering a visual-audible chord. Our identification of this new perception is a recognition of the synergy intrinsic to the event: we must contribute to, and inevitably complete, the performance; we provide the connective kinetic which brings the separate facets of the event through the manifold and into their own intellectual domain.

> (Imagination) takes apart the whole created universe, and, with the materials which it the gathers and reorders according to rules which originate in the deepest part of the soul, it creates a new world [...].[4]

Comprehending oral poetic performance on an individual, intellectual level has allowed its preservation through the generations in order to teach and reinforce the act of living. Oral poetics represents not only the artistic, but also the realistic necessities of tribal people — it is their daily bread. It is not an art to be enjoyed from the comfort of an armchair, or for an evening's entertainment — these are distinguishing characteristics of Western art forms. Oral poetic expression reflects

---

[4] Charles Baudelaire, *Salon de 1859*, ed. Jacque Crépet and Georges Blin, (Paris: Corti, 1949), p. 68.

and generates images from physical matter, from life, and from the realities of living on earth. Oral performance draws on and develops from a complexity of images, and for a Western audience demands the comprehension of a completely new language, a language, as Jean Dubuffet maintains, we *all* once possessed.[5] Oral performance eliminates the need for words to elucidate ideas and subjects relying instead on perception. The amalgam of language and gesture moves through space extending the limits of speech, and despite the fact that it is sustained for only a brief moment, locates life through this immediate act of performance.

> A scary choas fills the heart as 'spir'itual breath — in'spir'ation; and is breathed out into the thing-world as a poem.[6]

The very essence of oral poetry tears between antithetical contraries, the poet seeks to establish a system of analogies which, without suppressing tensions, resolves them into a harmony. This harmony strikes the highest function of the imagination, since it fuses analysis and synthesis, translation and creation. It is knowledge of and at the same time a transmutation of reality. Our sensibilities arch and engage different historical periods and civilizations as we spontaneously synthesize a bridge between languages, poetry, music, dance, and painting. This poetic promotes "the eternal" in that it articulates and traverses all times and all spaces in an image which, ceaselessly changing, prolongs and perpetuates itself each instant it strikes within our mind. This vital act transforms communication into creation and once again human consciousness emerges to engage the original moment of the naming act, and we experience the poetic word.

> The intention of such investigations is to plumb the depths of language and thought by drilling rather than excavating, so as not to ruin everything with explanations that seek to provide a causal or systematic connection.[7]

For oral poet, naming reconfigures and aligns human consciousness back into the fabric of an ecosystem which acts and lives. The language which separates the human from the earth finds and rejuvenates itself as we rediscover our primary tendencies toward language and living. Shattering the burdening shroud of solitude which human language creates, the poet resurrects and initiates other intelligences into our domain which liberate our unconscious selves. We escape our predicament and no longer witness our existence from the canopy of historical directedness framed by language which demands meaning. Human language is a construct

---

[5] Jean Dubuffet, *Anticultural Positions*, (Paris, 1949), p. 171.

[6] Gary Snyder, quoted in Ronald Gross and George Quasha, *Open Poetry*, (New York, 1973), p. 7.

[7] Walter Benjamin, *Briefe*, Vol 1, ed Gershom Sholem and Theodor Adorno, (Frankfurt/M.: Suhrkamp, 1966), p. 107.

though which humans perceive and understand the physical world, or what we call reality. The oral poet abandons this reality and attempts to move from past to present, from history imagined to nature experienced, from personal to universal, and from textual to mythic, acts which all re-establish dialogue between humans and certainty (nature).

No matter how we go about synthesizing the perceptions expressed by oral poetry, as we progress through it, there will be processes of anticipation and retrospection, along with a continual modification of attitudes and perceptions until a "knowing" or crystallized association ignites. This process of gathering perceptions and attitudes from a text clearly resembles and in fact parallels, the continual process of perceptual identification we exhibit in analyzing everyday phenomena. The actions involved in naming mimic phenomenological judgement.

> We have the experience of a world, not understood as a system of relationships which wholly determine each event, but as an open totality the synthesis of which is inexhaustible [...]. From the moment that experience — that is, the opening on to our "de facto" world — is recognized as the beginning of knowledge, there is no longer any way of distinguishing a level of a priori truths and one of factual ones, what the world must necessarily be and what it actually is.[8]

Whatever components we select, inspect, and bring into our consciousness enter as an result of our association with those elements. The governing factor of what information we possess and include into our consciousness focuses upon those perceptions or elements presented by oral poet which liberate us from associations of our own historical experience and knowledge of language and naming.

Both from the perspective of language and from that of history, the modern revolution in the arts have revitalized our concepts of expressive forms by promoting a search for language which can accommodate and privilege the discovering act revealed through the spoken poetic word. This urge to reconstitute and name, springs from an exhausted tradition which is over burdened with meanings and which can muster only a remanent of thought. This shift sparks a recognition of a language which although dormant has always been virtual and present. The core of this creation revolves around a flux existing between audience, experience, participation, provided by the artistic work. These fusioning activities transmutes into an expression which invites us to make immediate connections with the present, engaging a new language through naming. This activity places in jeopardy a language of traditional Western expression whose sum constitutes what has been called "humanism." The appeal is not an attempt to revive the living poetries of past cultures, but rather seeks to establish our present presence through the poetic possibilities provided by the poetic word.

---

[8] Georges Poulet, "Phenomenology of Reading", *New Literary History*, (Charlottesville, 1969), p. 55.

What is pure art according to modern conceptions? It means creating a suggestive magic
which contains both object and subject, the world exterior to the artist and the artist
himself.[9]

Whether we consider the original or the modern poetic "moment" we see that the
"word" is in conflict against itself. The word rests upon its historical representation rendered by the community, circumstance, occasion which sponsored its
genesis. Yet, what characterizes the poetic word resists its present historical
predicament and struggles to transcend its original placement. Poetic language
abandons words which abstracts meaning and which refers to a philosophical
world privileging historical objectivity. Poetic naming only signifies itself through
the act of poetizing, it names its present. Following this argument, poetry would
then become mute in that words would be unsayable, and yet what characterizes
the poem is its necessary dependence on the word as much as its struggle to
transcend it. The poetic word defies words and history, but the poem would have
no meaning without the history and the community that cultivates it and is
cultivated by it.

The poetic landscape illuminates a polarized world. On one pole, it provides
the self and the community a discourse of history. On the other pole, it denies
temporal placement by alerting the present. The language that initiates the poem
is nothing more than history, a name, reference, or meaning that is frozen in an
historical moment of the discourse of human consciousness. Yet, that very consciousness, at that moment, when life was breathed into its beginning, the naming
act gave birth to the present in an activity brimming with "meanings" that can
only be realized by way of its next call to existence. The original poetic moment
is not historical nor is it something that belongs to the past, it is always a virtual
presence.

Living as an incandescent moment, the poetic word prompts placement upon
its reception. The incandescence vital to poetic expression simultaneously concretizes a presence as it is both coming into and going out of existence. The
revelation of the poetic moment strikes our consciousness as we coalesce with the
poetic experience, and at that moment the poetic act is inseparable from its
expression. The poem is a mediation between the original experience and cluster
of subsequent acts and experiences, which only acquire coherence and meaning
in relation to the first experience that the poem consecrated though naming. It is
not an experience that language translates later, but rather the language itself
constitutes the nucleus of the experience. Until we baptize it, the experience lacks
existence. The poetic word is timeless, often we associate it with religious and
spiritual affirmation, since it always rests on a present while conjuring a presence.
Yet, the poetic word activates perceptual behavior rather than belief; giving shape

[9] Charles Baudelaire, *L'Art philosophique*, ed. Jacques Crépet, (Paris: Conrad, 1925), 185.

or form to the unconscious self, giving it imagery — essentially through the act of naming — the poet corrects the disorder of our physic shapeless worlds by physically conjuring our concrete selves into a concrete physical world. Unlike the world of philosophers and philosophies the poem does not abstract the experience, that moment is alway alive — the poetic word recovers the present.

Paulo Medeiros

Eating (with) Nietzsche: Reading as Devouring in *Die Fröhliche Wissenschaft*

SIGNIFICANTLY, A LARGE NUMBER of readers of Nietzsche has felt the imperative to question the very process of reading Nietzsche at all levels. *Reading Nietzsche* is the title of a collection of essays edited by Robert C. Solomon and Kathleen Higgins, where "reading" very properly describes the contents of the volume as a compilation of active readings of Nietzsche's various texts.[1] "Reading Nietzsche" is also the title given by Eric Blondel to the first chapter of his *Nietzsche: The Body and Culture* where it appears to be more a question than a statement.[2] This enunciation of a problematic of reading or of reading as a problem in itself is even more evident in the way J. P. Stern opens his essay on "Nietzsche and the Idea of Metaphor" ("How are we to read Nietzsche?"[3]), and in Gianni Vattimo's first chapter in his introductory book on Nietzsche: "Dalla filologia alla filosofia. Come leggere Nietzsche?"[4] Certainly the examples could be multiplied. Clayton Koelb, in yet another essay to question the process of reading Nietzsche in general, and especially in reference to *Die Fröhliche Wissenschaft*, points out that this line of questioning has been amply pursued by, among others, Paul de Man and Jacques Derrida.[5] Like Koelb, my intention is not so much to draw attention to the metaphoricity of Nietzsche's style, that is, the way in which rhetoric beyond being enmeshed with his philosophical arguments actually constitutes them, but rather to pursue a string of closely connected images frequently used by Nietzsche in association with reading, that can be subsumed

---

[1] Robert C. Solomon and Kathleen M. Higgins, eds. *Reading Nietzsche* (New York: Oxford University Press, 1988).

[2] Eric Blondel, *Nietzsche: The Body and Culture. Philosophy as a Philological Genealogy* [1986], transl. Séan Hand, (Stanford: Stanford University Press, 1991).

[3] J.P. Stern, "Nietzsche and the Idea of Metaphor," in: *Nietzsche: Imagery and Thought*, ed. Malcolm Pasley (Berkeley and Los Angeles: University of California Press, 1978), p. 64.

[4] Gianni Vattimo, *Introduzione a Nietzsche* (Roma: Editori Laterza, 1985), p. 3.

[5] Clayton Koelb, "Reading as a Philosophical Strategy: Nietzsche's *The Gay Science*," in: *Nietzsche as Postmodernist: Essays Pro and Contra*, ed. Clayton Koelb (Albany: SUNY Press, 1990), pp. 143–160.

under one expression: devouring. Images of consumption, references to diet, and above all incorporation ("Einverleibung"), proliferate throughout Nietzsche's texts in an obsessive manner. One would only have to refer to *Ecce homo* to understand the extent to which Nietzsche related eating to thinking. In "Warum ich so klug bin" the reader is treated to a discussion of Nietzsche's views on gastronomy that leaves no doubt that to him images of consumption are much more than mere tropes: "Ich verneinte zum Beispiel durch Leipziger Küche, gleichzeitig mit meinem ersten Studium Schopenhauers (1865), sehr ernsthaft meinen 'Willen zum Leben'[...]. Der deutsche Geist ist eine Indigestion."[6]

Indeed, one could look into Nietzsche's private life and find ample corroboration of his continuous interest in consumption, by itself, and in relation to his thought. In his letters to his family and friends he often commented on his diet and, in a letter to Heinrich Köselitz and a postcard to his sister (both dated April 10, 1881) he even exulted on a successful cooking attempt: " — Und noch etwas Heiteres: gestern habe ich auf meiner Maschine ein Genueser Gericht unter Anleitung meiner Wirthin gekocht, und siehe, es war vortrefflich" (*Briefe*, 84; cf. 83). He also made specific requests for certain food items that he prized, and once the request for a sausage is linked with writing itself: "Schreibt mir gute Dinge hier hinauf [...]. Auch eine äußerst delikate Wurst würde zu den guten Dingen gehören" (*Briefe*, 104). Most telling, however, is the direct correlation between thinking and self-consumption exhibited either in a remark to Erwin Rhode about intellectual solitude — "Ach, Freund, so muß ich denn fort und fort vom 'eignen Fette' leben: oder wie Jeder weiß, der dies einmal recht versucht hat, vom eignen Blute trinken!" (*Briefe*, 75) — or in a complaint to Köselitz about the oppressiveness of his own thought: "Aber vielleicht komme ich noch nach Venedig, etwa Mitte April, ich muß mich von mir selber abziehn, meine Gedanken fressen mich auf" (*Briefe*, 64).

Eric Blondel has extensively demonstrated how fundamental the body is in Nietzsche's thought, how "the metaphors of the body run into a body as meta-phor, an interpretative unity and plurality, in such a way that the body, used metaphorically in order to think of interpretation, is interpreted as interpretation."[7] A perfect example for this assimilation between body and interpretation is the passage Blondel cites from *Morgenröte* where Nietzsche explicitly refers to the text as a body.[8] Blondel, however, even as he accentuates the importance of the body, the physiological, and consumption in Nietzsche's thought, continues to strive for a differentiation between figurative and literal meaning. This attempt

---

[6] Friedrich Nietzsche, *Ecce Homo*, eds. Giorgio Colli and Mazzino Montinari, KGW 6.3 (Berlin: Walter de Gruyter, 1969), p. 277f.

[7] Eric Blondel, op. cit., p. 218.

[8] Ibidem, p. 119.

leads him to construct a hierarchical scheme whereby body metaphors are only building blocks towards something higher like interpretation — a question to be addressed further; and within the various types of images, those related to consumption are themselves only a first step towards more elevated, political, tropes.

In contrast, Malcom Pasley's earlier study of "Nietzsche's Use of Medical Terms," even though it does not advance the radical claims of Blondel, invites the reader to take Nietzsche's metaphors of consumption not only seriously, but even literally. In Pasley's view Nietzsche's use of physiological images start to cross the line between the literal and the metaphorical around 1875.[9] In reference to *Menschliches, Allzumenschliches* Pasley notes that Nietzsche "begins to concern himself directly with the body, with literal feeding habits [...]"[10] although "his metaphorical uses of [medical terms] proliferate [...] through mixing them with literal uses [Nietzsche] insinuates the idea that they can be understood literally as well." Such a practice — rather than paradoxical or inviting the devaluation of either, or even both, of the two terms, literal and metaphorical — must be seen as an acting out of Nietzsche's perspective on truth and language as formulated in his earlier essay "Über Wahrheit und Lüge im außermoralischen Sinn." As Koelb points out, there Nietzsche not only makes no distinction between truth and metaphor, since truth itself is composed by an army of tropes, but his very discussion of the issue is highly rhetorical.[11] Thus, in Koelb's view, Nietzsche's argument does not merely self-deconstruct, it also openly embraces that which undoes it (rhetoric) as its very essence, giving way to "a new discourse that actualizes both the literal and the figurative, both the assertion and its subversion."

Koelb's "Reading as a Philosophical Strategy" focuses on *Die Fröhliche Wissenschaft* as a "work which in several ways announces itself as the marriage of philosophy and poetry."[12] I would like to propose in this paper that it is precisely in *Die Fröhliche Wissenschaft* that Nietzsche's devouring stand is more obvious or more unavoidable, and that the strategy for philosophy as reading ultimately is a strategy of devouring. By "devouring" I do not mean simply a process of intertextual incorporation, although that too can be seen as part of Nietzsche's strategy. Even the way in which he cites Emerson in the opening epigraph, highlighting the relationship between the poet and the philosopher while silently eliding the saint, would indicate a certain "cannibalization" of Emerson, much in the same way that Nietzsche's appropriation and subversion of Goethe's lines in the concluding

---

[9] Malcolm Pasley, "Nietzsche's Use of Medical Terms," *Nietzsche: Imagery and Thought*, op. cit., p. 129f.

[10] Ibidem, p. 138.

[11] Clayton Koelb, op. cit., p. 145.

[12] Ibidem, p. 147.

poems does. By "devouring" I mean rather the way in which Nietzsche invites the readers to eat his text, and by extension himself.

Nietzsche opens *Die Fröhliche Wissenschaft* precisely with such a dare in the form of a poem:

Einladung.
Wagt's mit meiner Kost, ihr Esser!
Morgen schmeckt sie euch schon besser
Und schon übermorgen gut!
Wollt ihr dann noch mehr, — so machen
Meine alten sieben Sachen
Mir zu sieben neuen Muth.

How is the reader to take this invitation? Koelb has rightly pointed out the fundamental rhetorical nature of Nietzsche's assertions here, by concentrating on the play with the word "sieben" and how it is used both literally as a sign for increase and metaphorically as a deprecatory prefix indicating the triviality of the subject matter. Yet, the invitation is much more than just a playful wordgame, and its function goes beyond highlighting rhetorical strategies into forcing the reader to assume the position of eater of a text that is defined as a type of food for which one must first acquire a taste. Even "sieben Sachen" has to be read as referring on a literal level to the baker's "sieben Sachen" of the traditional children's song. That Nietzsche seriously intends to have the reader perceive his image literally, that is, without allowing the reader to simply accept the image of consumption as a rhetorical flourish, can be determined by his insistence on the act of devouring explicit in "Meinem Leser," where Nietzsche wishes his reader "Ein gut Gebiß und einen guten Magen."[13] In this poem too the connection between explicitly digesting the text and implicitly digesting, or agreeing with, its author is present: "Und hast du erst mein Buch vertragen, / Verträgst du dich gewiß mit mir."

Nietzsche seems to be saying that incorporating his text would provide a guarantee of affinity between reader and writer; an affinity that is modelled on incorporation, yet, by virtue of the changed case, shies away from explicit cannibalism. Why this reluctance, this resistance to present himself as fit for consumption by the reader, at the same time that he clearly wants to suggest such a possibility? Before attempting an answer it becomes necessary to specify in further detail the constellations around which consumption can be organized in and about Nietzsche's text.

The first, obviously, would be constituted by the references to consumption as a daily necessity, evidenced in the correspondence, as the examples mentioned above make clear. This, however, might not only be misleading but also mistaken.

---

[13] Friedrich Nietzsche, *Die fröhliche Wissenschaft*, eds. Giorgio Colli and Mazzino Montinari, KSA 3 (Nördlingen: dtb, 1969), p. 365.

For one, such references even as they characterize the correspondence, do not translate simply into Nietzsche's other writings, where images of consumption, although very important, are no longer presented as issuing out of daily concerns. Furthermore, even if one entertains the notion that Nietzsche's association of consumption with culture, for instance, is predicated precisely on his daily experiences, to insist on calling attention to the primacy of diet would simply replace one set of values, traditional aesthetics, morality, politics, with another, in a dichotomization that Nietzsche resisted as much as he was tempted by it.

At one point indeed Nietzsche considered the necessity to effect a reversal of values expressed in terms of an opposition between spirit and matter. In one of the 1881 fragments we read, "Veränderung der Werthschätzung — ist meine Aufgabe" followed by a series of terms, some in apparent opposition, at the top of which is "Der Leib und der Geist."[14] A similar list, still headed by those two terms under the rubric "Neue Werthschätzungen — meine Aufgabe" is also included in a larger list of pronouncements written in the summer of 1882.[15] Yet what this would entail is not so much a simple reversal of values, nor a debasement of spiritual concerns, but rather an attempt to avoid the common opposition between spirit and matter, and consider instead the impossibility to separate the two realms with any precision. In this respect, I would argue, Nietzsche's preoccupation with consumption and his valuation of it, goes beyond the simple attempt to replace values and strives for a questioning, if not abandonment, of the notion of value altogether as it is usually conceived, that is, in opposition to something other that would be valueless.

Blondel has carefully considered that point when he comments: "Nietzsche's metaphors on physiology are therefore not tangible images: they lead instead to the philological notion of interpretation. And it is in this way that these metaphors will not only constitute the *style* of *Nietzsche*'s descriptive meta-language, but also the interpretative status *of his object* itself; the body."[16] Whereas Blondel's view of the impossibility to separate the style of interpretation from the object of interpretation itself is essential for my understanding of Nietzsche's devouring stand, his reluctance to accord value to the images of consumption themselves, his view of them as intangible, appears problematic. Further in his argument Blondel seems to come to a decisive moment, when he asserts that,

> Moreover, if ontologically, Nietzsche maintains the body as a first reality, on the other hand, from the epistemological point of view (the only one he can support by virtue of challenging the in-itself), the ultimate principle is not the body, but

---

[14] Ibidem, p. 368.

[15] Ibidem, p. 581.

[16] Eric Blondel, op. cit., p. 205.

interpretation, the 'body' being merely the metaphor of interpretation, the human means of interpreting it. This leads Nietzsche, where we might expect a physiological reductionism, to deploy epistemologically a metaphysics of interpretation, whose 'physiological' discourse in reality is merely *metaphor*.[17]

Two aspects are noteworthy in this phase of Blondel's argument: one, the seemingly deprecatory qualification of "metaphor" through the reiteration of "merely." Blondel does not ignore Nietzsche's special deployment of rhetoric — his argument itself depends on it. Yet it becomes difficult not to imagine the supposition of something other that would either escape the taint of metaphoricity, or conversely, suffer from its lack. Linked to this is the mention of a hypothetical expectation for "physiological reductionism," which Nietzsche averts. This aversion, however, is only possible because Nietzsche's discourse always reveals itself as metaphor. At this point it is tempting to consider whether Nietzsche's reluctance to have his text (and himself) devoured by the readers might not provoke a corresponding anxiety in the readers. To maintain that if Nietzsche's images of consumption had slipped from strict metaphoricity his discourse would have implied a consequent reductionism is to acquiesce precisely to the system of valuation that Nietzsche sought to undermine. Such an implicit standard is also what allows Blondel at another point to subsume Nietzsche's "'medicynical' phrases" under the rubric of "burlesque" or satire and to view their author as yet another follower in a long tradition from Aristophanes to Heine.[18]

The other problem in Blondel's assessment concerns his division of Nietzsche's images of consumption into an ontological and an epistemological level. It is not so much the apparent contradiction in Blondel's position — oscillating between a relegation of Nietzsche's metaphors to the level of a none too novel sort of burlesquerie and a consideration of the philosophical import of those same images — as the difficulty inherent in attempting to separate the epistemological from the ontological in reference to Nietzsche's views on consumption. Nietzsche's use (and abuse in Blondel's view) of images of eating and drinking and their concomitant physiological results to think through cultural issues in general and in particular forms another, and more important, constellation.

Within this constellation it is necessary to differentiate between simply satirical (although no less acute) observations and the complex process by which Nietzsche both refers to consumption metaphorically to understand cultural development and insists on thinking of politics, morality, and art literally as extensions of physiological acts. When he explicitly enjoys word games such as, "Ridicultur eines Menschen / der geistige Nachtisch jetzt für viele: Gorgon-Zola" [19], one can

---

[17] Ibidem, p. 218f.

[18] Ibidem, p. 228.

[19] *Werke*, 5.2, p. 476.

enjoy the subtle approximation effected between the emphasis placed on human decay by Naturalism and the cheese's characteristic corruption; or one can also enjoy the linguistic economy of excess evident both in the conflation of two words into one ("Ridicultur"), or the exploding of one word into three ("Gorgon-Zola"), but Blondel's portrayal of Nietzsche as satirist would appear confirmed. However, even in relatively simple and short speculative passages such as the one where Nietzsche questions the very notion of cultural progress to admit only of culinary progress,[20] it is clear that Nietzsche's object is not so much, or at all, the devaluation of a "higher" term ("Kultur") through a direct comparison with a "lower" one ("Küche"), but rather a re-thinking of the two; or as he says, "Den Begriff der Ernährung erweitern."[21]

This expansion of the meaning of consumption does take an ontological and an epistemological configuration as Blondel points out. Assimilation becomes the process by which change is effected and just as Nietzsche at one point considers the body as the key for change (" ... der Sitz der Veränderung in der Physis ist"[22]) so consumption becomes the model for other human activities: "Der Eigenthumstrieb — Fortsetzung des Nahrungs- und Jagd- Triebs. Auch der Erkentnistrieb ist ein höherer Eigenthumstrieb."[23] And just as Blondel seems to note, even as he privileges the epistemological function, consumption is given a decidedly ontological character by Nietzsche, evident throughout *Die Fröhliche Wissenschaft* and even more so in the corresponding fragments of 1881 and 1882.

Such a direct correlation between consumption and ontology should not be taken to mean that at this period Nietzsche entertained a materialist perspective. One would have only to compare Nietzsche's observations with those of Brillat-Savarin or Feuerbach. It is clear that Nietzsche did not accord to consumption the pleasure value that led Brillat-Savarin to write what would become a model for future essayists on the subject of consumption, the *Physiologie du goût*. One could say that where Brillat-Savarin tried to bring a philosophical perspective to the consideration of consumption, Nietzsche was intent on bringing the notion of consumption into philosophical discourse, assimilating it but also causing some violence in the process.

Brillat-Savarin's famous statement on the ontological significance of consumption, "Dis-moi ce que tu manges, je te dirai ce que tu es," however, is often approximated by Nietzsche's argument.[24] Nonetheless, Nietzsche stopped short of such a sweeping identification between the consumed and the consumer.

---

[20] Ibidem, p. 374.

[21] Ibidem, p. 339.

[22] Ibidem, p. 376.

[23] Ibidem, p. 357; cf. 388.

[24] Jean Anthelme Brillat-Savarin, *Physiologie du goût* (Lausanne: Pierre Waleffe, 1967).

For instance, in a series of fragments from 1881 Nietzsche ponders on the nature of Being ("Sein" or "esse"), which he brings back into his notion of "Irrthum"[25] as the central principle for cultural change. The assimilation of "Grundirrthümer" is presented by Nietzsche precisely as the first step in the "Versuch" of what would become one of his main ideas — the notion of eternal return. There the role ascribed to assimilation is clear: "Die Wiederkunft des Gleichen. /Entwurf./ 1. Die Einverleibung der Grundirrthümer./ 2. Die Einverleibung der Leidenschaften. / 3. Die Einverleibung des Wissens und des verzichtenden Wissens. (Leidenschaft der Erkenntnis)."[26] In the passages where Nietzsche directly speculates on the nature of Being though, assimilation is not mentioned.

Feuerbach, who gave a new twist to Brillat-Savarin's aphorism with the equally famous pronouncement that "der Mensch ist, was er ißt" did take the ontological validity of consumption seriously ("Wie die Speise, so das Wesen, wie das Wesen, so die Speise," "Das Geheimnis des Opfers."[27] One can certainly see an approximation between the two thinkers even if Feuerbach in a footnote to the essay where he develops his controversial statement represents himself as "ein ganz schrecklicher Materialist" ("Das Geheimnis des Opfers."[28] This approximation depends much on the fact that for the two consumption was a way of approaching central cultural problems and that both focused on issues of religion and morality.

Whereas Feuerbach was intent on understanding the nature of religious action and thought through a concentration on the rituals of offerings of food and drink to divinities thereby placing Judaism and Christianity in line with other religions, Nietzsche was more interested in pursuing and denying Christianity (and Judaism as Christianity's origin) and traditional morality. Nevertheless, the center of Feuerbach's interest — in the form of ritual sacrifice — was also related to Nietzsche's concerns and might just serve as a basis for understanding Nietzsche's reluctance to "offer" himself completely to his readers. In Feuerbach's terms, "Opfern heißt die Götter speisen"[29] and precisely many of the particular aspects of sacrifice examined by Feuerbach, such as salt and blood, appear in Nietzsche's considerations in the 1881-82 fragments, although in not altogether clear form. With this in mind, and remembering the ontological-epistemological importance

---

[25] *Werke*, 5.2, p. 464ff.

[26] Ibidem, p. 392.

[27] Ludwig Feuerbach, "Die Naturwissenschaften und die Revolution" [1850] and "Das Geheimnis des Opfers oder Der Mensch ist, was er ißt" [1862]. *Schriften zur Ethik und nachgelassene Aphorismen*, ed. Friedrich Jodl (Stuttgart: Frommann, 1960), p. 43.

[28] Ibidem, p. 41.

[29] "Das Geheimnis des Opfers", op. cit., p 50.

accorded to consumption by Nietzsche one can better evaluate the initial question of Nietzsche's reluctance to equate himself with his book as items of consumption.

Perhaps the tension that becomes evident in *Die Fröhliche Wissenschaft* between wanting to dare the reader to a quasi-literal devouring of his text and the refusal to let the same strategy apply to himself beyond inference can be explained by reference to one possible model for the type of textual devouring that Nietzsche invites us to perform. The command to eat the text is a divine command, whereby the literal ingestion of scripture by the prophet is meant to lead to a proper assimilation of its meaning resulting in a more effective propagation of the divine will. For instance, the passage in Ezekiel is among the most explicit:

> "But you, son of man, hear what I say to you; be not rebellious like that rebellious house; open your mouth, and eat what I give you." And when I looked, behold, a hand was stretched out to me, and lo, a written scroll was in it; and he spread it before me; and it had writing on the front and on the back, and there were written on it words of lamentation and mourning and woe. And he said to me, "Son of man, eat what is offered to you; eat this scroll, and go, speak to the house of Israel." So I opened my mouth, and he gave me the scroll to eat. And he said to me, "Son of man, eat this scroll that I give you and fill your stomach with it." Then I ate it; and it was in my mouth as sweet as honey. (2:8-3:3, 1002)

At the level of taste there is a direct correspondence between the scroll with its bitter content, the "words of lamentation and mourning and woe" and Nietzsche's text which is also tough to bite into and hard to digest, and whose taste is not immediately appreciated. However, what is most striking is the inversion of values and attitudes that Nietzsche's invitation performs. Instead of the stern command to eat the scroll so that the eater, Ezekiel, might then properly speak with God's words instead of his own (3:4), Nietzsche presents a playful if malicious dare for the reader to eat his text, not so much to have his words replace those of the reader but to provoke the reader into his own. This is very explicitly stated in further poems in "Scherz, List und Rache" such as "Interpretation"[30] and "Vademecum-Vadetecum" where the reader who is attracted by Nietzsche's style and speech ("Es lockt dich meine Art und Sprach") is counselled to follow himself rather than the author if he is to follow the author at all.[31]

Moreover, even the direct correspondence between scripture and Nietzsche's text that could be elicited on the grounds of both items being bitter at first, and then turning agreeable upon being consumed, is misleading, because although the

---

[30] *Werke*, 5.2, op. cit., p. 357.

[31] Ibidem, p. 354.

divine Logos is in itself a message of woe, Nietzsche's words are the opposite. They are supposed to reflect an excess of hope and joy, which Nietzsche refers to as a "Trunkenheit der Genesung."[32] In Nietzsche's own judgement in *Ecce Homo*, *Die Fröhliche Wissenschaft*, like *Morgenröthe*, is foremost a positive, hopeful "jasagendes Buch." This does not mean that Nietzsche thinks ingesting his text is easy nor that he shuns advising the ingestion of repelling substances. Indeed, to those pessimists who continuously complain of never finding anything to their taste Nietzsche expressly prescribes a horrific diet as cure: "Folg mir, mein Freund! Entschliess dich frei, / Ein fettes Krötchen zu verschlucken, / Geschwind und ohne hinzugucken! — / Das hilft dir von der Dyspepsei!"[33] In the same vein, Nietzsche's praise of Julius Bahnsen's texts, which he explicitly refers to as anti-pessimistic food ("Kost") and which he declares he has used in that manner, turns them into a laxative for the most constipated of bodies and minds alike.[34] Yet, in reference to his own text, it would seem that Nietzsche would prefer rather to employ a discriminatory and refined taste, which he maintains is the attribute, as well as the danger, of those who are most happy ("Gefahr des Glücklichsten").[35]

The tension between the seduction of presenting his text for the reader's devouring and withholding himself from becoming such an offering at the same time can be further interpreted as a tension between the seduction of excess and the resistance to sacrifice. In his commentary on stoicism and epicureanism Nietzsche works out this tension in an exemplary way. On the one hand, it would seem that the practice of devouring repellent and harmful substances as an antidote to nausea, would be recommendable and even comparable to Nietzsche's own proposition in writing *Die Fröhliche Wissenschaft* out of his suffering and pain; on the other hand, it is the discriminatory and minimalist practice of the epicurean that Nietzsche praises and ascribes to all those who work with the spirit, because of a need to preserve one's capacity for stimulation.[36]

If one were to consider a further extension of the divine command to eat the incarnate Logos, that is, the Eucharistic message, perhaps one could then interpret Nietzsche's tension as a resistance to transform himself into, or have others interpret him as, yet another Christ figure. Curiously enough, Nietzsche never alludes to that one paradigm of textual incorporation, the literal/metaphorical devouring of the word made flesh, yet his one reference to cannibalism in *Die Fröhliche Wissenschaft* does raise the question of whether Nietzsche avoided

---

[32] Ibidem, p. 346.

[33] Ibidem, p. 358.

[34] Ibidem, p. 601.

[35] Ibidem, p. 541.

[36] Ibidem, p. 545.

presenting himself more explicitly as food precisely because of the danger implicit in such an extension of the invitation to devour his text. In "Misanthropie und Liebe" Nietzsche proposes that, "Man spricht nur dann davon, daß man der Menschen satt sei, wenn man sie nicht mehr verdauen kann und doch noch den Magen voll davon hat. Misanthropie ist die Folge einer allzubegehrlichen Menschenliebe und "Menschenfresserei' ..."[37] In equating the love for man with cannibalism, Nietzsche is still cautious enough to put "Menschenfresserei" within quotation marks as if to prevent any too literal a reading of that image, even as the rest of the passage seems to emphasize its literalness. The excess referred to here is a negative one, another form of indigestion that paralyses and consequently reverses love into hate. The only reference to cannibalism in the 1881-82 fragments emphasizes the "spiritual" aspect of cannibalism as the reason for its condemnation as taboo: "Man aß das Fleisch nicht, weil man nicht die Seelen von Menschen verspeisen wollte, es war also nur ein Abscheu vor der Menschenfresserei..."[38]

The problem with the passage in "Misanthropie und Liebe" is two-fold: first, it seems that to Nietzsche such a cannibalistic practice of love is condemnable, and in this he could be seen as rejecting the Eucharistic model whereby men symbolically devour Christ so that "[h]e who eats my flesh and drinks my blood abides in me and I in him" (John, 6:56, 1296). Christ's sacrifice is explained as one of love and takes the form of a mutual incorporation, however figurative. It is perhaps as a reaction against this model that Nietzsche both admits his own "cannibalism," when he says "Ah!, wie schwer sind die Mitmenschen zu verdauen"[39] and condemns it.

The second problem with the passage on misanthropy is that Nietzsche is only too ready in other places not only to imagine himself as devourer, but also to emphasize the necessity of hunger when conceived of as desire. This is precisely the tenor of "Bei der dritten Häutung," where Nietzsche as snake appears to celebrate the continuation of an excessive type of eating, "Zu essen Das, was stets ich ass, / Dich, Schlangenkost, dich, Erde!"[40] Nor is Nietzsche loath to present himself as autophagy, when as in the poem on "Ecce Homo" he maintains,

Ja! Ich weiss, woher ich stamme!
Ungesättigt gleich der Flamme
Glühe und verzehr' ich mich.
Licht wird Alles, was ich fasse,

---

[37] Ibidem, p. 499.

[38] Ibidem, p. 441.

[39] Ibidem, p. 364.

[40] Ibidem, p. 355.

Kohle Alles, was ich lasse:
Flamme bin ich sicherlich.

This poem recalls the way in which Feuerbach discusses Jehovah and consumption: "Ist Essen oder Fressen nicht ein heute noch überall vorkommendes, für uns alle freilich nur noch bildliches, für den die Natur aber verpersönlichenden und vergötternden Menschen im eigentlichen Sinne geltender Ausdruck von Feuer? Heisst und ist nicht Jehovah selbst ein verzehrendes, wörtlich: essendes oder fressendes Feuer?"[41] The marking difference, however, is in the direction of the flame's consumption, which in Nietzsche's poem obliterates the distinction between subject and object, consumer and consumed.

In the light of such poems and reading strategies as contained in *Die Fröhliche Wissenschaft* and the 1881-82 fragments, or the even more explicit ontological pronouncements of *Ecce Homo*, one might want to rethink Blondel's consideration of Nietzsche's fascination with images of consumption. Instead of seeing devouring solely as a metaphor for interpretation, I would like to propose that at least in the example of *Die Fröhliche Wissenschaft*, devouring and interpretation appear as interchangeable practices, that reading is always a devouring for Nietzsche; and that, even if Nietzsche was highly ambivalent about the value of such devouring, he nonetheless was obsessed by it. This obsession and ambivalence is perhaps nowhere stronger than in his remarks against idealism, where he conjectures that "Philosophieren war immer eine Art Vampyrismus."[42]

---

[41] "Das Geheimnis des Opfers", op. cit., p. 49.

[42] *Die fröhliche Wissenschaft*, op. cit., p. 624.

John Rice and Paul Malone

Text or Performance:
The Rationalism and Intoxication
of Presence in the Theatre

IN AN ATTEMPT TO ESTABLISH an understanding of the "Semiotics of Theatrical Performance," Umberto Eco takes up C.S. Peirce's questioning of the sign-making processes defined by the putting on stage of a drunken man. As soon as he is placed before an audience, the drunken man loses what Eco refers to as "his original nature of real body among real bodies."[1] He becomes a sign or semiotic device, "something that stands to somebody for something else in some respect or capacity, a physical presence referring back to something absent."[2] Eco's semiotic inquiries leave one with the idea of the text as a written code which not only precedes, but is the same as — and therefore intends — the meaning of the staged sign. The text, for Eco, does more than just pre-exist the performance; it is not just a map, "a blueprint which persists from enactment to enactment," indicating a variable pattern of events,[3] it also controls the "meaning" behind the performance. In order for the meaning of performance to be repeatable, the location of meaning must be sought in something both permanent and original, i.e. the dramatic text. The success of the sign-in-performance becomes, in effect, little more than a function of the extent to which it fulfills and completes its "true" referent, the sign-in-the-text.

If this were really the case, however, it would be difficult to see what might be the source of that "sudden epiphany of intoxication" which Eco correctly identifies as the "basic mystery of [good] theatrical performance."[4] The contradiction here is obvious: once Eco has framed the staged sign in its dramatic, theatrical, and socio-ideological contexts, however, he leaves it there in a kind of temporal isolation from other potential performance elements. Its meaningful context is that

---

[1] Umberto Eco, "Semiotics of Theatrical Performance," *Drama Review*, Vol. 21, 1, (1977), p. 110. See also: Charles S. Peirce, *The Collected Papers*, Vol. 2 (8 Vols., Cambridge, Mass., 1931-58), p. 135ff.

[2] Eco, op. cit., p. 110.

[3] Richard Schechner, "Theatre. Performance. Script. Drama." *Drama Review*, Vol. 17, 3 (1973), p. 5-36.

[4] Eco, op. cit., p. 110.

of the absent referent, and in effect, we are not required to think of the sign-in-performance in the context of a full dramatic performance. If we are going to better contextualize the relationship of text and performance in the theatre, we clearly need a more refined and realistic set of *starting definitions*.

Roland Barthes, for example, describes theatricality in a more complex manner: the theatre is a "cybernetic machine" allowing the spectator to receive "at the same time six or seven items of information (proceeding from the set, the costumes, the lighting, the placing of the actors [onstage], their gestures, [and] their speech)."[5] Barthes sees the actor in a contextual relationship which better reflects the realities of theatrical practice. He emphasizes that these six or seven sign systems do not operate identically, but in rhythmic counterpoint: some remain more or less constant throughout a performance (e.g. the set), while others change continuously (speech, gesture, etc.). Barthes' list of communicative elements does not in fact include the text as playscript at all, but only the words as spoken by the actors. Nevertheless, the question which we inherit from his investigation remains a significant one: if the words, like the actors' gestures, are changing constantly during the performance, does the text from which they speak remain unchanging?

This "density of signs,"[6] the polysemy of theatre, has long been recognized by semiotics. In enumerating the multiple sign systems of theatre, Barthes' successors were more careful to list the text as document and the verbal signs of the performance as *discrete elements*.[7] For example, Jean Alter describes the theatrical event as an artistic experience which works within and between its two basic categories of signs:

> As a text it presents a network of verbal signs which usually appear in the form of plays made of written words, and involve primarily linguistic, but also literary and cultural codes. As a performance, it offers a network of many types of signs which, in addition to words, include body language, costumes, sets, lights, colours, props etc., each type belonging to a discrete code, and all of them [...] involving common theatrical and cultural codes.[8]

In order to be considered somehow "complete," the theatrical production of a dramatic work must fulfill a dual need, i.e., the need for a relatively permanent form without which it cannot be maintained, and the need for a concrete presenta-

---

[5] Roland Barthes, *Critical Essays*, trans. Richard Howard (Evanston: Northwestern UP, 1964), p. 261.

[6] Barthes, op. cit., p. 262.

[7] Martin Esslin, *The Field of Drama: How the Signs of Drama Create Meaning on Stage and Screen* (London/New York: Methuen, 1987), p. 52-3.

[8] Jean Alter, "From Text to Performance: Semiotics of Theatricality," *Poetics Today*, Vol. 2:3 (1981), 113-4.

tion of the dramatic work in performance. This dual need has led to often violent debate on the issue of priority between text and performance in the theatre: where is the location at which meaning is generated in the theatre? Where should dramatic analysis base its interpretive efforts? What is the role of the director in dramatic production? In attempting to answer these questions, the central issue has frequently been formulated, not in terms of "text *and* performance," but in terms of "text *or* performance."

In the latter case, the two possible locations of meaning are perceived as mutually exclusive. On the one hand, there is what might be called the "textual scheme" of interpretation. The text is something which survives as the permanent notation of the author's dramatic vision (of his or her word), and which therefore validates itself as the permanent and unchanging notation of that vision; a vision which the performance represents, but which it can never hope to repeat as itself. Performance is, at best, little more than a partial interpretation or translation of the essential body of the text. Understanding the theatre remains a function of the sign-in-the-text, and the essence of theatricality is assimilated into a special branch of literature.[9]

At the opposite pole of interpretive possibilities is the "performance scheme." The dramatic vision of the play is intended as a living language, to be witnessed not in the notation of signs in a text, but as the living, constantly changing interaction of signs-in-performance. This vision — the play — is incomplete, even meaningless, without the transformation into performance of the textual document. Performance is, in effect, "substituted for the text, [which is] reduced to the status of a pre-text, and hence equivalent to all other staging signs."[10]

The tradition of theatre in Western culture has so long been dominated by the text, by the written word of the dramatist, that the text might seem the natural or original location of meaning for performance. But as such critics as Bernard Dort and Richard Schechner have pointed out, outside of post seventeenth-century drama in Europe (and the strongly European-influenced cultures of North America and Australia), the text is more commonly subordinate to the staged production than vice versa.[11] The privileging of the dramatic text in post-Enlightenment theatre is reluctantly acknowledged by Jacques Derrida, who refers to it as a

---

[9] The idea of textual and performance schemes in our paper owes much to Jean Alter's discussion of the "literary and performance fallacies" (Alter, op. cit., p. 114-6) in the analysis of drama.

[10] Alter, op. cit., p. 115.

[11] Richard Schechner, op. cit., p. 18-36; Bernard Dort, "The Liberated Performance," trans. Barabara Kerslake. *Modern Drama*, Vol. 25, 1 (1982), p. 60-61.

"verbal fabric, a logos which is said in the beginning,"[12] the utterance of an author whose dramatic vision the textual scheme would have us maintain in its original form. The authority of the text, then, is a function of the authority of the author, and like Barthes, Derrida views this phenomenon of the "Author-God" as a product of the humanist emphasis on individuality that has emerged in the Occident since the late Middle Ages.[13]

Alter, on the other hand, describes the privileging of the text in Western theatre tradition in terms of a kind of semiotic transfer which is specific to theatre/drama among the performance arts:

> Verbal signs in the text are repeated as verbal signs in the performance, [...] and they retain their linguistic code although their materiality changes from graphic to sounded signifiers. The autonomy of the text reflects the (erroneous) belief nurtured by the [textual] fallacy, that the *referents* of the verbal signs are not modified by this transition from text to stage, and hence that reading may be substituted for hearing and seeing.[14]

At issue here are not two mutually exclusive schemes of explanation for the dominance of the author/text in Western theatre. That is: it is not a case of replacing a socio-historical investigation of theatrical tradition with a semiotic analysis of the special relationship of signs in the theatre. Rather, it is hoped that the combination of the basic insights and methodologies of these two approaches will help to arrive at an understanding of the ideologically loaded history of the dramatic sign, of the complex interpretive issues and ambiguities of which the sign (both on page and stage) can perhaps only carry a trace, but which cannot be removed from the paradigm which makes up the signification of that sign. From the moment when theatre became the *exclusive communication* of the individual dramatist, and ceased to be the *manifestation* of the community who both created and watched the performance,[15] theatre in the Western tradition has been involved in, and continues (to a large extent) to involve itself in a struggle — whether through the privileging of the text, or through a "return" to the privileging

---

[12] Jacques Derrida, "The Theatre of Cruelty and the Closure of Representation," *Writing and Difference*, (Chicago: Chicago UP, 1978), p. 235.

[13] Roland Barthes, "The Death of the Author," *Image, Music, Text*, trans. Stephen Heath (New York: Hill & Wang, 1977).

[14] Alter, op. cit., p. 114-5. A similar change of materiality takes place between the notational signs of music and choreography on the page, and their sounded or visual forms in performance. In the cases of music and dance, however, the notational language is highly specialized, and very few people — with the exception of experts — have occasion to pre-read the performance in this form. The unique and specific nature of the theatre lies in the fact that the notational language of the playscript is so commonly understood. Alter's claim is that many more people read plays and literature than actually attend performance on a regular basis.

[15] Schechner, op. cit., p. 7.

of the performance as the site of meaning — to establish a self-present meaning; to find a form of communication through which it can locate and express its message in its "original wholeness."

> The concepts of quality and value — and to the extent to which these are central to art, the concept of art itself — are meaningful, or wholly meaningful, only within the individual arts. What lies between the arts is theatre. [...] The success, even the survival, of the arts has come increasingly to depend on their ability to defeat theatre.[16]

These are the conclusions of Michael Fried: if the dramatic text must advertise the necessity of its being embodied in more than just its own notation in verbal signs, and the performance cannot help but refer back to a script (or other absent referent), then — Fried claims — the theatre must by definition refuse all "notions of essential form"[17] in art. The mediation of the text through the agency of performance serves only to distort the poetic art of the playwright, and to obscure the clarity and signification of form. Performance is, in effect, a "regressive manifestation of no interest,"[18] which, insofar as it encompasses a multiplicity of different possible affective interfaces, can do nothing but "complicate, diffuse and displace the concentrated self-identity of a work of art."[19]

Theatre lies in a unique semiotic position between text and performance, between *product* and *process*,[20] and it is precisely this to which Fried objects. His search is for a definable centre in the text, a structuring principle which controls the artistic form or meaning of the work-in-itself, free from the interference of audience or topical context. When Fried claims that art "degenerates as it approaches the condition of theatre,"[21] this reflects a structuralist approach of the most fixed, essentialist kind. The work-of-art-in-itself is seen as something which transcends, or is fixed, outside the individual; that which is variable in theatre is rejected, and the idea of presence is firmly established in the *logos*, which can repeat itself without loss or contamination of meaning. In other words:

---

[16] Michael Fried, "Art and Objecthood," *Artforum*, (June 1967); rpt. *Minimal Art: A Critical Anthology*, ed. Gregory Battcock (New York, 1968), p. 139-142.

[17] Steven Connor, *Postmodern Culture: An Introduction to Theories of the Contemporary* (Oxford: Blackwell, 1989), p. 133.

[18] Chantal Pontbriand, "The Eye Finds No Fixed Point on Which to Rest," trans. C.R. Parsons, *Modern Drama*, Vol 25, 1 (1982), p. 155.

[19] Connor, op. cit., p. 133. It should be noted that in both this and the previously cited work, the respective authors restate Fried's argument in criticism of his position, and not in agreement with it.

[20] Ibidem, p. 133.

[21] Fried, op. cit., p. 141.

the word both contains and is able to transmit the "purity" of the author's artistic intent.

The paradox of this is clear: the meaning of the work is fixed in an artistic-linguistic centre, and yet the individuality and authority of the creating author — who must, by definition, be separate from the centre — is not called into question. Where does the authority of the individual come from, to locate, collate, and express meaning, to communicate that which can be considered not only valid, but "true"? Fried argues, somewhat tautologically, that this authority belongs to the *logos*, the "language tradition" in which the author places both him- or herself and the would-be self-present meaning of his or her text.

But, as both Norris and Culler state — following Barthes' cynical analysis of the language *tradition*, and Derrida's deconstruction of the *language* tradition — the metaphysics of presence "runs deep in the logic and communicative structure of language"[22]; so deep indeed that to explore the boundaries of linguistic presence is to risk either madness or unintelligibity. Meaning requires a consistent repetition, without which it could not establish itself in an ontological frame of reference and signification. Instances of presence in language are "already complex constructions"; language is a social phenomenon without essential meaning. That which is proposed as "an elementary constituent" proves in fact to be "a product, dependent or derived in ways that deprive it of the authority of simple or pure presence."[23] Truth is, in effect, little more than a mobile army of rhetorical devices and metaphors,[24] an "honorific title assumed by the argument which has got the upper hand."[25]

The idea of the *logos* (the word of the author) as the carrier of meaning is possible only with the deferral of the individual's authority to, and its ultimate location in, a more or less universally accepted (or "higher") authority or tradition, a tradition which might be socio-culturally, ethico-politically and/or religiously determined. We might call this a *rationalized presence*, for it involves the simultaneous recognition and forgetting of socio-linguistic conventions as being essentially natural. In any event, it is necessary to emphasize that there is nothing either natural or inevitable about the authority of tradition, nor about the relationship of the individual author to that tradition.

This is not to suggest that the individual author is totally subordinate to the controlling forces of a repressive tradition, as might be implied, for example, by

---

[22] Norris, op. cit., p. 57.

[23] Jonathan Culler, *On Deconstruction* (Ithaca: Cornell UP, 1982), p. 94.

[24] Herbert Blau, "Ideology and Performance," *Theatre Journal*, Vol. 35, 4 (1983), p. 456; Blau quotes Nietzsche in English translation from "Wahrheit und Lüge im außermoralischen Sinne." Here we borrow Nietzsche's military metaphor from Blau's translation.

[25] Norris, op. cit., p. 60.

a Marxist model. Marx writes in his *Remarks on the New Instructions of the Prussian Censors* (1842): "The Law permits me to write, it asks only that I write in a style other than my own. I am allowed to show the face of my mind, but first I must give it a prescribed expression." Although we cannot entirely agree with Marx, we may still make use of the kernel of his complaint: it is not simply the content of the author's discourse which must be placed in an ideological context, it is also the form by which means the author structures his or her argument. Herbert Blau has raised the point that all the communication media (including theatre) are involved in an ideological struggle over the signification of events; a struggle "not only [over] the right to life, but the right to determine its meaning."[26] In other words: it is not just the question of what is thought, but the issue of how that thinking process takes place, which is ideologically determined.

Fried's attempt "to restore art to itself by detheatricalizing it,"[27] — to establish an absorbed and self-present meaning-in-the-text as the central principle of the artistic form — is clearly impossible. Language is not capable of supporting the purity and specificity of form that Fried demands from "artistic value." All thinking — as Nietzsche would remind us — is "always and inseparably bound to the rhetorical devices [the indicative limitation of language] that support[s] it."[28] The logocentric rationalism of presence (i.e., of the author's word as an expression of truth in the theatre) is betrayed not, as Fried might suggest, by the mediation or interference of performance, but through the impossibility of self-present meaning in language *per se*. Derrida's acknowledgement of the author's central role in Western theatre is not intended as an affirmation of the author's will to speech, but as the basis for a deconstructive criticism of a theatrical tradition in which the text or verbal language has been privileged to such an extent that the director and actors, as well as all the other elements of performance, have become little more than "interpretive slaves who faithfully execute the providential designs of the master."[29]

It is precisely this tradition of the authority of the logocentric text as the basis of theatre which Artaud rebelled against in developing his "Theatre of Cruelty"

---

[26] Blau 1983, op. cit., p. 457.

[27] Connor, op. cit., p. 136.

[28] Norris, op. cit., p. 60-1; in traditional discourse, the power of rhetoric is treated with suspicion; it is thought (a) to possess "neither reason nor moral self-knowledge", and (b) "to lend itself to uses that are ethically indifferent."

[29] Derrida 1978, op. cit., p. 235.

in the 1930s.[30] At the heart of his cry for an explosive theatre of ancient ritual — an Oriental theatre of concrete languages[31] where the "overlapping of images and movements will culminate [...] in a genuine physical language with signs, not words, as its root"[32] — was the violent rejection of French theatrical traditions, which since the neo-classicism of the seventeenth century "had overglamorized the spoken word and tended to reject [de-emphasize] all physical action."[33]

For Artaud, this tradition amounted to nothing less than the prostitution of the idea of the theatre. He explicitly announced the intention of the "Theatre of Cruelty" to "put an end to the subjugation of the theatre to the text"[34] and to "renounce the theatrical superstition of the text and the dictatorship of the writer."[35] The Western tradition of theatre — as far as Artaud was concerned — had effectively worked towards the suspension of itself as theatre. A performance or stage whose purpose it was simply to represent the wishes of an absent author, to fulfill the signification of the signs in the text, or to repeat itself unthinkingly in the illustration of another's discourse, could no longer be — in Derrida's words — "entirely a stage."[36]

Artaud's vision was to absolve performance from the burden of its secondary status. The *mise-en-scène*, rather than existing merely as "the degree of refraction of a text upon the stage," was to become "the point of departure for all theatrical creation."[37] The tacit agreement which had for so long given priority to the language of words above all others was now broken; the theatre no longer had to limit itself to the requirements of this one language, but could discover its own (independent) signifying functions in the languages of gesture, movement, lighting, music, masks and rhythm. The performance was — in other words — to become

---

[30] Connor refers to Artaud's theatrical emphasis on performance as a "desperate struggle against the belief in the full and perfect embodiment of thought in language, and the structures of repetition that guarentee it, with the stage always acting as the supplementary shadow of original full speech." Connor, op. cit., p. 139.

[31] Antonin Artaud, "The Theatre of Cruelty," *The Theatre and its Double*, trans. Mary C. Roberts (New York: Grove Press, 1958), p. 56.

[32] Artaud 1958, op. cit., p. 68.

[33] Richard Hornby, *Script into Performance: A Structuralist View of Play Production*, (Austin: Texas UP, 1977), p. 57.

[34] Artaud 1958, op. cit., p. 55.

[35] Ibidem, p. 66.

[36] Derrida 1978, op. cit., p. 236.

[37] Artaud 1958, op. cit., p. 59; in his article on Artaud's "Theatre of Cruelty and the Closure of Representation," Derrida explains the former's vision of the mise-en-scène in the following terms: performance was no longer to "re-present a present that would exist elsewhere and prior to it, a present whose plenitude would be older than it, absent from it, and rightfully capable of doing with out it: the being-present-to-itself of the absolute Logos." (Derrida 1978, op. cit., p. 237.)

the site at which the theatre re-discovered its true value in its "excruciating, magical relationship to reality and danger," a relationship which, if properly explored, would "uncover the notion of a kind of unique language half-way between gesture and thought."[38]

If Artaud rejected the idea of the verbal language as the self-present carrier of meaning, he did not, however, abandon the search for a self-presence of meaning *per se*. Instead, he re-located the potentiality of self-present meaning from its "traditional place" in the text to the *intoxication* (the immediate presentness) of the sign-in-performance, the performed sign in the act of becoming on stage.

Artaud speaks of creating a "naked language" in the theatre, a language which is not virtual (indicative) but real, and will therefore flow directly into the sensibility of the audience.[39] Unburdened by either a past (textual authority) or by a future (once performed, the sign-in-performance can never be repeated as itself), the performed sign simply takes place. In the instant in which they are presented, the multiple signifiers of a performed sign disappear. The distortion of meaning, which Fried had objected to in the idea of performance-as-repetition, is viewed by Artaud as a function of the text-as-*logos*. Only the text can be repeated, thereby opening itself up to possible distortions; each performance, on the other hand, creates itself anew!

The language of words was not to be cast out entirely from Artaud's new theatre; rather, they were to become only one part of his "passionate equation between Man, Society, Nature and Objects."[40] The vital task of the theatre was to find a language capable of "organically re-involving man, his ideas about reality, and his poetic place in reality."[41] Artaud denied the role of words in theatre only to the extent that they had been the theological dictation of the author.[42] It was intended, instead, to return the spoken language to its originary sensual physicality, so that it — alongside all the other sign-systems of the theatre — could communicate directly, not through a series of abstracted associations. Words were to be given "approximately the importance they have in dreams."[43] The "Theatre of Cruelty" sought to embrace a language of ideas which could

---

[38] Artaud 1958, op. cit., p. 55.

[39] Ibidem, p. 57.

[40] Ibidem, p. 56.

[41] Ibidem, p. 58.

[42] "The stage is theological for as long as it is dominated by speech, [...] for as long as its structure, following the entirity of tradition, comports the following elements: an author-creator who, absent and from afar, is armed with a text and keeps watch over, assembles, regulates the time or meaning of the repre-sentation, letting the latter represent him as concerns [...] his thoughts, his intentions, his ideas" (Derrida 1978, op. cit., p. 235).

[43] Artaud 1958, op. cit., p. 59.

touch on "Creation," "Becoming," and "Chaos."[44] In other words: what Artaud sought to express was the power of a deep inner reality, a poetic essence of life which was present in the truth of dreams,[45] and which could provide the audience with a transcendent vision of Truth and Life. As Artaud put it, his aim was "to create a metaphysics of speech, gesture and expression, in order to rescue [the theatre] from its servitude to psychology and human interest."[46]

Artaud's desire to restore the theatre to its true self creates what Connor describes as an "aesthetic of impermanence."[47] His is an attempt to present (not *re*-present) a point of origin independent of any framework of repetition.[48] In escaping the restrictive structure of the logocentric tradition, however, Artaud's emphasis on the performative materiality of language places his argument in an equally essentialist tradition of metaphysical discourse, with its roots in Socratic phonocentrism. Rather than construct a discourse dependent on the malleable rhetoric of written language, this tradition privileges the voice/spoken word, which — because of the immediacy with which spoken signifiers disappear once they have been sounded — has been credited with being somehow "closer" to the original point of meaning.[49]

As with Fried, we are faced here with a metaphysical impossibility. All language — however preconditioned or spontaneous; however involved in, or removed from, the structures of repetition it may appear to be; whether written, spoken or performed; whether purely verbal, or incorporating a multiplicity of sign-systems — must always simultaneously create, exist within, and derive from a complex play of significations. Performance is just an alternative form of language; and it is not just the graphic representation of the written word which *differs* and *defers* from its signified. Neither, in answer to Fried, is it just the representative mediation of performance which is subject to the deconstructive play of *différance*. Artaud's physicalization of theatrical language, rather than achieving its ideal of a "unique, continuous, presentational form [...] signifying

---

[44] Ibidem, p. 56.

[45] Artaud raises the dream above its substitutive psychological function (where it is a refraction of the individual personality) to an exalted status, where it becomes a true expression of the reality or essence of life (Artaud 1958, op. cit., p. 58-9).

[46] Ibidem, p. 56.

[47] Connor, op. cit., p. 134.

[48] Derrida points out that Artaud's "historico-metaphysical decision" was to erase repetition on the basis that "repetition seperates force, presence and life from themselves" (Derrida 1978, op. cit., p. 245); note that the French *répétition*, used by both Artaud and Derrida, means not only "repetition," but also "rehearsal" — that process in which, as Peter Brook has pointed out, actors often learn to perform unthinkingly and theatre thus becomes "deadly." See Peter Brook, *The Empty Space* (Harmondsworth: Penguin, 1972), p. 153-7.

[49] Culler 1982, op. cit., p. 89-95.

meaning only in overall configuration,"[50] is obliged in effect to encounter the point at which it is a derived language of signs, reflecting attitudes and ideologies in the same way as the written word or text of the author.

Fried's total privileging of the text, and Artaud's apparent rejection of the authority of the text in favour of performance; Fried's attempt to protect the essence of the work from repetition, and Artaud's desire to strip the repetition of performance from its dependence on essence; both, in effect, come down to the same thing, i.e., the attempt to absorb and fix a self-present meaning into a language of the stage. Each wishes to produce a "finished product" (or "finished process") which is complete in itself. And, while Artaud's "Theatre of Cruelty" is clearly the more "powerfully subversive act"[51] — insofar as it specifically undermines the dominant tradition of the theatre as the domain of the author — it does so only in order to establish another site of absolute authority.   Artaud himself never advocated such ideas as collective or free improvisation in performance, nor did he intend to include the audience in any form of direct participation.[52] His was a theatre of discipline and control, and the site of this control was the director, Artaud: "[My plays are not] left to the caprice of the wild and thoughtless inspiration of the actor [...]. I would not care to leave the fate of my plays and of the theatre to that kind of chance."[53] In the interest of protecting his creations from "caprice" and "chance," Artaud wished to record his performances for posterity by means of "musical transcription or some sort of code," a code made up of "hieroglyphic characters."[54] Artaud's desire to create an artifical polarity between the text-in-performance and gesture (two sign systems which, in usual theatrical communication, overlap with and are dependent on one another[55]) blinds him to the fact that the "code" he hopes to create is equally a text. The creative function of the author is thus usurped by the creative desires of the director, and in the latter instance — as in the former — the sign-in-performance is an authoritative textual statement.

Not only do Fried's and Artaud's respective positions — occupying the polar extremes of the textual and performance "schemes" — constitute a "metaphysical impossibility," but they also show themselves to be theatrically impracticable. Anyone privileging the text to the extent that Fried does would hardly be likely

---

[50] Hornby, op. cit., p. 58-9.

[51] Connor, op. cit., p. 139.

[52] See Hornby, op. cit., p. 57.

[53] Artaud 1958, op. cit., p. 109-10.

[54] Artaud 1958, op. cit., p. 59.

[55] Keir Elam, *The Semiotics of Theatre and Drama* (London: Methuen, 1980), p. 73.

to involve him- or herself in the production and performance of a dramatic text; whereas followers of Artaud have often sought to remove the theory and practice of performance even from the theatre. The perception of polarity as existing at all ("text *or* performance") has begun slowly to give way, in the last two decades, to a realization that text is already inherently performance, and that performance is already inherently a text — by virtue of their status as tactical constructs, made up of linguistic and/or performative (gestural/spatial) strategies. The moment on stage when "text *and* performance" meet and mingle is what is described in postmodern theatre as the play of intertextuality[56]; where the performance-as-signifier both limitlessly extends, and fails to exhaust, the text-as-referent. It is — we suggest — this varying state of tension between "separate" but equal and interdependent texts (or performances) which is, to the contemporary practitioner and onlooker, the source of Eco's idea of theatrical intoxication.

The interdependence, the "collusion between text and performance" which Dort posits as the essence of theatre,[57] is essential (in Dort's terms) not only as a formal compromise required by the restrictions of the theatrical genre, but also — and more importantly — because it is only when the text and performance are placed in counterpoint to each other that they are able to mutually deconstruct the myth of presence which the other seeks to establish. The question of an authoritative location of meaning is put aside. Such is not to be found, even in the process of translation or transformation required between the page and stage. Rather, the performance sets itself up as a critical reworking and questioning of the text, while the signification of the text is maintained as the source of this reworking, whose role it is both to question and to be questioned.

---

[56] See, e.g., Fred McGlynn, "Postmodernism and Theater," *Postmodernism, Philosophy and the Arts*, ed. Hugh J. Silverman (New York: Routledge, 1990), p. 148.

[57] Dort, op. cit., p. 60.

Louis F. Helbig

Lessing's Psychogony
as a Theory of Spiritual Culture

THIS ESSAY APPLIES the well-known Augustinian motto which prefaces Lessing's *Erziehung des Menschengeschlechts* — "For the same reasons, this is all in a certain sense true, and in a certain sense false"[1] — to the alleged true or false nature of the soul-principle in that work. It can be called true, for example, that "Seele" plays a major role in German thought during the latter half of the eighteenth century, and it is also true that in Lessing's famous piece, which was published in 1780, the motto assumes a key function, albeit often misunderstood. The principle of soul-migration, for example, has often been declared false reasoning out of hand, in order to cast doubt on Lessing's thought as a whole, both on theological as well as philosophical grounds.

An additional aspect is important within the context of the *Erziehung des Menschengeschlechts*. It consists of a limited drawing into account, beyond rather incomplete references to soul-migration, of one of Lessing's short essays, namely "Daß dem Menschen mehr als fünf Sinne sein können," which was written in 1778.[2] Although caution seems advisable in this regard because, for one thing, that piece did not reach the public until Lessing's brother published it posthumously, it appears fully justified to make this essay and its claims the cornerstone for the present undertaking. On the other hand, it seems reasonably certain that the argument to be forwarded here should become more readily acceptable, if one realizes that the inner logic of Lessing's thought is at stake, not only influence or reception, or references to historical place and time.

For those reasons it would be false to judge the present experiment in thought ('Gedankenexperiment') by any other criteria than that it is just that: an ex-

---

[1] Gotthold Ephraim Lessing, "The Education of the Human Race," tr. by Henry Chadwick, in: *Nathan the Wise, Minna von Barnhelm, and Other Plays and Writings*, ed. Peter Demetz (New York: Continuum, 1991), pp 319–334. All quotations refer to this edition. Throughout this paper references are made to my own edition: *Gotthold Ephraim Lessing. Die Erziehung des Menschengeschlechts. Historisch-kritische Edition mit Urteilen Lessings und seiner Zeitgenossen, Einleitung, Entstehungsgeschichte und Kommentar*, Hg. v. Louis Helbig (Bern: Lang, 1980).

[2] Gotthold Ephraim Lessing, *Werke*, Bd. 8 (München: Hanser, 1979), pp. 557–560. All quotations refer to this edition (translation mine).

periment. As for its results, neither their true nor their false nature is to be judged in what follows; instead, nothing less — or more — than Lessing's conceptualization of thought-possibilities ("das Denkmögliche") will carry weight. This establishes a connection with the hotly debated, though by no means resolved issue of Lessing's status as a philosopher.

Given those premises, it appears promising to determine the degree of plausibility inherent in Lessing's notion of the individual soul, especially to what extent its governing principles resemble those perceived as determining the system of the cosmos. We shall ask whether there is a parallelism between cosmogony and psychogony expressing itself in a uniquely Lessingian concept of spiritual culture. In order to assess the validity of those assertions, it seems wise to first reappraise Lessing's philosophy before returning to his spiritual world model.

Lessing's importance as a "religious thinker" as based on his theological writings has been recognized with unrelenting frequency for a number of decades.[3] Upon closer scrutiny one can readily discover, however, that religious thought is not always distinguished sufficiently from philosophical thought. In short, the issues in Lessing's thinking are categorized either as 'merely theological' or, in a manner which resembles a topos in Lessing research, as one attempt after another to find fault with both aspects, calling it 'not sufficiently systematic as a body of philosophical thought.' However, those days appear over when philosophies were taken seriously only if they appeared in highly structured Kantian or Hegelian systems, and so the time has come to judge Lessing on the basis of the essential value of his thought.

Taking into account the longevity of this topos and bearing in mind the philosophical — not: theological — nature of the topic under investigation, one probably does well nevertheless by starting out with the observation — true or false — that Lessing indeed has not produced a coherent system of philosophy. We are, of course, somewhat less concerned about such coherence than were Lessing's contemporaries. For us it suffices to acknowledge that — system or no system — his philosophical problems, ideas, and approaches can be seen as being more or less coequal in validity. For this reason one should not exclude from consideration Lessing's so-called "faith in reincarnation" — usually the litmus test for much of the older literature on Lessing — by labeling that faith, if indeed it was no more than that, as untypical or even irrelevant on the grounds that it allegedly played only a minor role in Lessing's philosophy. The fact that he had chosen himself not to develop a so-called system of philosophy is conveniently forgotten by the very same interpreters.[4]

---

[3] Cf. Manfred Durzak, *Poesie und Ratio — vier Lessing-Studien* (Bad Homburg: Athenäum, 1970), esp. p. 105ff.

[4] This position is taken, for example, by Christoph Schrempf, *Lessing als Philosoph*, 2. Aufl. (Stuttgart, 1921), p. 190.

Therefore, the intention cannot be to define, as did Friedrich Schlegel, "Lessings Geist im Ganzen,"[5] "Lessing as an individual,"[6] or "als religiös existierendes Subjekt,"[7] nor his "Weltanschauung."[8] Similarly, this is not the place to develop his philosophical stance, as Wilhelm Dilthey has done, by postulating "Lessing, the philosopher" from an assumed "moralischen Seelenverfassung der deutschen Aufklärung,"[9] or, like Martha Waller, by comparing "Lessings Geisteshaltung" with those "für die Zeit konstitutiven Gedanken," with the predictably meager result which tells us what we knew all along: that Lessing was a "Kind seiner Zeit."[10] Therefore, instead of interpreting Lessing's approach against the background of a larger concept such as the Enlightenment or another biographical or historical context, an effort is made to single out one aspect of his thinking: his understanding of what he calls "soul," or "the soul," and its significance for what the eighteenth century did not know as a concept, namely a *theory of culture*.

Before taking this next step it is important to remember that Lessing's philosophical approach was essentially critical, not "schwärmerisch." By oscillating between religiously motivated "revelation" ("Offenbarung") and enlightened "education" ("Erziehung") his thinking was never fully rational, because it was always conscious of its irrational components. What makes him unusual and innovative for his time is precisely that he is never unaware of the dangers of irrationality, but that he dares to think forward nevertheless, unimpeded by hesitation dictated by religion, or mandated by rationality in an increasingly secular state of enlightenment.

His thinking was directed toward overcoming the immobility which characterized both the moral edifice of church teachings as well as the descriptive conquest of the culture. From an early stage in his career he was on the lookout for a concept which he would be able to use to explain culture, its state of being at any given time, and its processes of change over time. This concept can be found in his essay on the human senses: "Daß mehr als fünf Sinne für den

---

[5] Friedrich Schlegel, "Über Lessing," in: *Ausgewählte Werke*, Hg. E. Sauer (Berlin, 1922), p. 151.

[6] Joseph Schmitz, *Lessings Stellung in der Entfaltung des Individualismus* (Berkeley, 1941), p. 142.

[7] Otto Mann, *Lessing: Sein und Leistung*, 2. Aufl. (Hamburg, 1961), passim.

[8] Hans M. Wolff, *Die Weltanschauung der deutschen Aufklärung in geschichtlicher Entwicklung* (München, 1949), p. 241ff.

[9] Wilhelm Dilthey, *Das Erlebnis und die Dichtung. Lessing, Goethe, Novalis, Hölderlin*, 13. Aufl. (Stuttgart, 1957), p. 79.

[10] Martha Waller, *Lessings "Erziehung des Menschengeschlechts"* (Berlin, 1935), p. 166.

Menschen sein können" ("That there may be more than five senses for human beings").[11]

The question whether or not there are more than five senses is not simply a rhetorical one. What matters is where and how each sense was added to the human faculties, and whether or not this might happen again. For Lessing there seems to be no doubt that this 'shift' or 'quantum leap' could happen at any time. Therefore he dedicated much of his thinking toward defining the type of sense quality which would be added 'next time.' For all one can gather, it seems that the new sense would combine moral awareness with a new historical perspective. No doubt, this had to be considered heretical by the theological estblishment of Lessing's time. Eitel Timm's book, *Ketzer und Dichter*, shows convincingly through a number of examples how Luther's "Schwärmerei," Goethe's predilection toward "Innerlichkeit" as well as "Pietismus," and Lessing's interest in "Frei-maurerei" are representative, in an escalating manner, of the "individuelle Rebellion des Sturm und Drang": undoubtedly, they were heresy, because all those attitudes went against everything public, including the state and the churches, while being supportive of the individual soul.[12]

Lessing's works are characterized by this spirit of rebellion, and the two examples discussed here are no exception. If state and church expect the individual to perform like a celestial body in an orderly cosmos, thus Lessing might have thought, then I must demonstrate that it is 'thinkable' as well as 'plausible' that the human soul, or psyche, may find a more compatible place for experiencing "Offenbarung" and "Erziehung" in a structure organized in accordance with a soul-principle. That is the point in the present discussion where the term 'cosmogony' demands a matching term which one may call a 'psychogony.'

It hardly needs to be said that *cosmogony* is used to describe various models explaining the origins of the universe as a system of celestial bodies — masses of matter which revolve around each other in accordance with the laws of physics. By analogy, the term *psychogony* alludes to the notion of a cosmos held together by the laws of the psyche, or soul, as well as the self.[13] It is clear, of course, that

---

[11] Lachmann/Muncker, as cited in *Werke*, Bd. 8 (München: Hanser, 1979), pp. 557–560.

[12] Eitel Timm, "Der Ketzergedanke und die individuelle Seele", in: Eitel Timm, *Ketzer und Dichter. Lessing, Goethe, Thomas Mann und die Postmoderne in der Tradition des Häresiegedankens* (Heidelberg: Winter, 1989), pp. 48–58.

[13] In the absence of definitions for "psychogony," a comparison with "cosmogony" seems helpful: "Kosmogonie, Lehre von der Weltentstehung, urspr. in mythisch-dichterischer Form bei nahezu allen Völkern vertreten (meist Schöpfungsakt einer Gottheit); später naturwissenschaftliche Auffassungen und Ergebnisse über die Entstehung des Weltalls. In den Vordergrund getreten ist die auf die Relativitätstheorie gestützte Vorstellung, daß der Anfang der kosmologischen Entwicklung gleichbedeutend mit dem Zeitbeginn ist." In: *Brockhaus in zwei Bänden* (Mannheim, 1984), Bd. 1, p. 642.

this expresses only two possible interpretations which the physical and the humanistic sciences have developed over time. But while government agencies such as NASA are still busy exploring with the intent to prove the accepted notion of the origins of the universe, there can be no denying that, generally, efforts of soul-searching must continue along less spectacular lines. It remains to be seen which goal will turn out to be the one that is less elusive. One reason — a minor one, of course — may lie in the fact that only very few soul-treatises have tried to reconcile the limited existence of one human being with the vastness of time. Lessing's contributions to such efforts, his 22-paragraph statement on "revelation" to the senses and his 100-paragraph manifesto on "education," have not been considered as commentaries on the development of humankind, only as odd pieces without clear intent.

By psychogony, then, I mean a cosmogonic concept based on a soul-principle. It tries to capture the idea — Lessing's idea — that the creation and development of the world occurred not only according to the laws of physics, but of ethics and moral responsibility as well. This is to suggest that a psychogony is a cosmos codetermined and perhaps governed by "souls," soul-entities, or soul-forces. It suggests further that one should be able to formulate and prove as viable equations such as these:

1. "revelation" ("Offenbarung")   = manifestations of culture
2. "education" ("Erziehung")   = memory building
3. "memory"   = tradition
4. "tradition transfer"   = cultural transfer

— with the 'chain of being' easily extendable to become a model for the totality of a 'process of culture,' both insofar as individuals and societies are involved. Again, Lessing stops short of rounding out this model. But its key elements are there: What is 'revealed' to the human eye — in a secular sense, of course — is 'what is,' and human being are becoming of aware by learning; awareness of development over time leads to the concept of tradition, reinforced by an ever changing stream of manifestations of culture; finally, but only as the end of one single cycle, there is giving and taking, and sharing.

The second paragraph of *Die Erziehung des Menschengeschlechts* addresses these aspects: "Education is revelation coming to the individual man; and revelation is education which has come, and is still coming, to the human race" (§ 2). One may read this as: Education, as a predestined experience, is the process of enculturation by which individuals become members of their culture, whereas revelation, as the sum of all manifestations of a given culture [in the sense of 'manifestations revealed'], thus includes all individual and universal [i.e. collective] human achievements. This suggests that both education and revelation are neither only spiritual, nor only physical, but that the two together were Lessing's — and his contemporaries' — way of addressing cultural development in a logical, progressive way: First, the individuals become adapted to their cultural environment (enculturated), and secondly, it is the environment which expresses that collective effort. It, forever manifesting itself in new configurations, then influences each individual. Whether or not the individual soul reaches immortality according to a divine plan or by default, or not at all, was the main concern when Lessing was alive. Today, it must no longer be considered as the key issue. However, since Lessing's notions seem to be much more modern than has so far been assumed, at least the argument ought to be discussed. In many cases this may become the point of departure for individual access to Lessing's ideas.

This brings us back to the crucial point: What *is* Lessing's idea of the soul? This much seems certain: It would be inappropriate in view of the inherent historical dimension to entertain only its psychological dimension. Lessing was not a modern psychologist. Taking his brief essay, "That there may be more than five senses for human beings," as a key statement, it has become clear why it is sensible to choose this essay with its almost absurd title as a take-off point for our argumentation. Its often-quoted first sentence, "The soul is a simple entity capable of limitless imagination" ("unendlicher Vorstellungen fähig"), implies equating it with consciousness itself, which, as any post-Enlightenment philosopher will confirm, is that "bundle of perceptions" of the British empiricists ascending to ever higher levels of apperception. Order is the principle that prevails, and indeed: "Its principle of order and measure are the senses," thus the essay which hypothesizes that there may be more than five.

This is what Lessing has done: He lessened the importance of their number by postulating a continuum of an increasingly complex consciousness. From this argument must follow that five may well be a preliminary, not the final number. Five senses are tentatively acceptable ('vorläufig-zureichend'), not ultimately sufficient ('endgültig-hinreichend').

There is a long tradition among Lessing's interpreters which calls this argument "Sophisterei" or, worse, "Vernünftelei." However, the argument may also be seen as a more dynamic, evolutionary monadology than Leibniz' whose monads were 'windowless.' Leibniz answered the problematics of singularity and multiplicity, consciousness and identity, humankind and evolution with a mathematical *tour de force*, but still evasively when insisting on his famous prestabilized harmony. Lessing's psychic monads are precisely not 'fensterlos.' In his unobtrusive and often overlooked sketch on the senses, Lessing actually transgresses the limits which Leibniz introduced and Kant did not dare to ignore: the limits of human thought and human knowledge. It is for this reason that Lessing's thought never could be forced into a system, even if he had chosen to do so, because it had to keep its windows open, so to speak. "That is why one must not draw into question the possibility of a sixth sense and more," he says, "as one should not doubt the possibility of a fifth, if we had only four senses." This is the core of Lessing's plea that there may be more than five, and that those thoughts presuppose the "system of pre-existing souls and metempsychosis." Virtually all interpreters find themselves in agreement with Lessing on this point: from Herder to Hans Leisegang, Martha Waller, Kuno Fischer to Ernst Krieck. However, there is no clarity regarding the important differences between the many related, though by no means identical principles: "Seelenwanderung," migration of souls, metempsychosis, pre-existence of the soul, and others more.

It simply does not seem practical to dismiss this notion categorically as "Schwärmerei," neither would it be useful to assume that Lessing himself 'believed,' or 'did not believe,' in the pre- and post-existence, or, in a religious or philosophical sense, the *immortality of the soul*, by drawing assurances from the Christian, Ancient Greek, Persian, or Buddhist-Indian belief systems.

Some recent studies come very close to raising the issue under consideration here, but they fall short of doing so.[14] Thus, Eitel Timm does discuss heresy and the individual soul, as already acknowledged, but mostly in relation to *Sturm und Drang* and Goethe, but not beyond; however, he deserves credit for the most appropriate term "psychonautische Ketzer," but seems to reserve it for Kierkegaard and Nietzsche, not Lessing.[15] Looking across the landscape of Lessing research, it appears that Ernst Krieck's approach is the one which, based on Lessing's crucial concepts of "revelation" and "education," provides the kind of help needed at this point. Krieck touches upon the root of the problem which virtually all those who discuss metempsychosis do not seem to see, namely that a soul entering a reincarnated state from a pre-existing one would not necessarily remember its earlier reincarnations. It is that aspect of remembering — the function of memory in culture — which Lessing does in fact address in § 99 of *Die Erziehung des Menschengeschlechts*: "Is this the reason against it? Or, because I forget that I have been here already? Happy is it for me that I do forget. The recollection of my former condition would permit me to make only a bad use of the present. And that which I must forget *now*, is that necessarily forgotten for ever?"

This appears to be the answer to Lessing's question: 'I have not forgotten it, if that which I seem to have forgotten forever during the course of many incarnations comes back to me in a future incarnation because of a developing sixth sense.' This, phrased more precisely, is the key hypothesis at the end of *Die Erziehung des Menschengeschlechts*, if one takes into account the statement on the senses. Those two pieces are conjoined into one statement at the point where memory becomes crucial. The ability to remember is meaningful in two ways: for the individual, because thus the immortality of each soul might become provable,

---

[14] The most recent example is Horst Möller, "Erziehung des Menschengeschlechts," *Vernunft und Kritik. Deutsche Aufklärung im 17. und 18. Jahrhundert* (Frankfurt/Main: Suhrkamp, 1986), pp. 133–144.

[15] Eitel Timm, *Ketzer und Dichter*, op. cit., p. 82ff.

and for society at large, because this is what collective memory means and where cultural continuity and tradition become operative. Here, then, are the cornerstones of Lessing's theory of culture.

Although this may be difficult to prove within the scope of this presentation, the argument put forth is that, instead of short-circuiting Lessing's concepts of "revelation" and "education" with theology or mystic speculation, they should be connected with *culture*. What is 'revealed' to each and every human being, and thus society, is made up of all the manifestations of culture at a given place in time, and "education" constitutes all individual and collective efforts of becoming aware of the *process of culture*. In other words, Lessing is presenting a surprisingly modern model of the system of culture. Although based on spiritual culture (it has to be that because he starts with the soul), it includes — at least conceptually — the physically manifested realm of culture as well, and it is a complete model because of its teleological dimension. As such it addresses the crucial aspect of continuity by including a mechanism for the survival and transfer of cultural experiences, for each human being as well as for humankind as a whole. In this lies the philosophical significance of *Die Erziehung des Menschengeschlechts*. Together with the essay "That there may be more than five senses for human beings," Lessing has given us a theory of spiritual culture, not only *in nuce*, but *sub specie aeternitatis et realitatis*. His model, once justly considered, could provide a broad perspective which points far into the future.

Compare this with a typically negative, philistine interpretation. Quoting Erich Schmidt: "Die von jedermann gefühlte Bizarrerie seiner Ansichten über die Zahl der Sinne fällt nicht sowohl der Idee der Metempsychose zur Last als der mathematischen Künstelei, den absonderlichen, unwahrscheinlichen Voraussetzungen arithmetischer Kombinationen."[16] What Lessing is offering is neither bizarre nor improbable. It may be unfamiliar, but that is the waking call we hear also from other parts of his work cosmos. Least of all can Lessing's "Gedankengang" be called "vollkommen durchsichtig," which is what Schmidt suggests.[17] There can be no doubt that Lessing never offers easy solutions, but he is not a sophist either. He often challenges us into an effort of trying to disprove his argument, an effort which itself tends to become an exercise in sophistry.

Are there any interpretations which do justice to Lessing's concept of the individual psyche as a key building block of his model? As far as one can judge, only Martin Bollacher's *Lessing: Vernunft und Geschichte*[18] deserves credit in

---

[16] "The bizarre nature of his ideas about the number of the senses, which is felt by everyone, cannot be attributed to metempsychosis, but rather to mathematical acrobatics and arithmetic combinations which are as weird as they are improbable." Schmidt, op. cit. p. 416 (my translation).

[17] Ibidem, p. 443.

[18] Martin Bollacher, *Lessing: Vernunft und Geschichte. Untersuchungen zum Problem religiöser Aufklärung in den Spätschriften* (Tübingen: Niemeyer, 1978).

this respect. He is careful to point out that "what arouses those feelings of alienation and uneasiness among modern readers" should not obscure our view of Lessing's educational model to the point of making it seem noncommittal, rather that the truth of his hypothesis, which consists of history and reason being one, should be understood as confirming the likelihood of the notion of soul-migration as a viable philosophical alternative.[19] This notion together with Lessing's speculative expansion of the human sense faculties, although somewhat "fantastic" even in Bollacher's view, appears to him as the framework ("Schema") of "a *paidagogia Naturae*, a progessive expansion of everything conditioned by nature."[20]

At this point, it is the notion of progress which reestablishes the interconnectedness of nature and culture in Lessing's thought model. Passed along in the unfolding history of consciousness, there now appears "a structured pattern of Lessing's concept of tradition" ("ein Muster des Lessingschen Traditionsverständnisses"), a pattern which includes the psychogonistic notion of the soul, or psyche, as the link between the individual and the universal, between each age and the continuum of culture.

In the realm of culture, it is often unclear to what extent analysts are able to see the difference between the education of an individual ('die Erziehung des Menschen') and the education of humankind ('die Erziehung der Menschheit'). Even when the differentiation is made, the role and function of education is often seen only as the secular progression of revelation. Revelation, history, education, evolution, and the development of culture are not just symptoms of ongoing changes in human consciousness, they are themselves constituent factors of change.

Although Lessing's argument is based on the spiritual principle of the human soul, its intent and application is practical. Hence the somewhat surprising point, because it sounds quite traditional, in the *Erziehung des Menschengeschlechts* that Christ was "the first reliable, practical teacher of the immortality of the soul" (§ 58). Why "practical"? Because Lessing was careful not to make a mistake similar to the one made by most of his contemporaries, namely by staying so close to orthodox theology that his philosophy, like theirs, could just as well be ranked among the teachings of the main churches. Lessing's psychogonistic model and its practical consequences for the individual in the social-cultural context, which he had to explicate in terms of a soul among souls, may therefore be ranked favorably among similar early attempts during the eighteenth century to create a *pre-modern theory of culture* in the making.

In summary, these observations on the subject of "Lessing's Psychogony as a Theory of Spiritual Culture" seem to demand clarification as to the extent

---

[19] Ibidem, p. 327.

[20] Ibidem. p. 331.

Lessing's model could be considered as a *paradigmatic core of a theory of culture*, a concept of culture comprising cultural manifestations as well as processes. Everyone appears to share a good part of the apprehension and often dissatisfaction with the seemingly endless (and often fruitless) perambulations across the soul-migration territory in the literature dealing with Lessing. In sharp contrast to those discussions there is a feeling of excitement over what — in spite of its sketched form — appears to be more than a mere draft of a theory of culture, a theory which as such Lessing did not develop, but whose building blocks can be found in his work and therefore should not be ignored.

Having reached this preliminary conclusion, it may be said that the parallelism between a cosmogonistic and a psychogonistic worldview has indeed been shown to be operative in the writings examined. Lessing's understanding of culture as a system has as its guiding principle not so much the external structures of society and state, but of the individual soul and its ethical responsibility which transcends any individual's lifespan. Following Lessing's example, the continuing process of education of the human race can now be pursued in a more encompassing sense than suspected: in a practical, ethical, and spiritual sense.

Index